Enchantment of the World

FRENCH GUIANA

By Marion Morrison

Consultant for French Guiana: George I. Blanksten, Ph.D., Professor Emeritus of Political Science, Northwestern University, Evanston, Illinois

Consultant for Reading: Robert L. Hillerich, Ph.D., Professor Emeritus, Bowling Green State University; Consultant, Pinellas County Schools, Florida

CHILDRENS PRESS ®
CHICAGO

The canoes carved by the Wayana Indians are dried over fires.

Project Editor: Mary Reidy
Design: Margrit Fiddle
Photo research: Judy Feldman

Library of Congress Cataloging-in-Publication Data

Morrison, Marion
    French Guiana / by Marion Morrison.
        p.   cm. – (Enchantment of the world)
    Includes index.
    Summary: Discusses the geography, history, people,
economy, and customs of *La Guyana*, an Overseas
Department of the Republic of France.
    ISBN 0-516-02633-X
    1. French Guiana–Juvenile literature.   [1.   French Guiana.]
I.   Title.   II.   Series.
F2448.5.M67   1995
966.52–dc20   94-37950
                                                            CIP
                                                             AC

Picture Acknowledgments
AP/Wide World Photos: 50 (right), 69 (2 photos)
Bettmann: 92
The Bettmann Archive: 32, 36, 50 (left), 52

© **D. Donne Bryant Stock:** © **J. P. Courau,** Cover, 12, 24
(inset), 56, 74 (top and bottom left), 76 (left), 106
© **Victor Englebert:** 8, 28, 47, 49 (left), 74 (bottom right), 75
Ivy Images: © **Brian Beck,** 20 (left)
North Wind Picture Archives: 29 (right)
Photri: 79
© **Porterfield/Chickering,** 49 (right)
South American Pictures: 31, 38, 47 (inset); © **Guyanese
Space Centre,** Cover Inset, 80, 102; © **Tony Morrison,** 4, 5,
6, 10, 13 (2 photos), 14, 15, 16, 18 (2 photos), 20 (right), 21
(right), 24, 34, 44, 59, 61 (2 photos), 62 (2 photos), 63, 64
(2 photos), 66 (right), 68 (right), 72 (top and bottom), 76
(right), 77, 78 (2 photos), 81, 82, 83, 84, 85, 86, 87, 89, 90
(2 photos), 91, 92, 97 (2 photos), 98, 99, 104, 105, 108, 111,
112; © **Corinne Peignon,** 94, 95 (2 photos)
Stock Montage: 29 (left)
SuperStock International, Inc.: © **T. Linck,** 23 (left); © **Dr.
Nigel Smith,** 23 (top right); © **A. Mercieca,** 26 (left)
UPI/Bettmann Newsphotos: 48 (2 photos)
Valan: © **Wayne Lankinen,** 19 (inset); © **Rob & Melissa
Simpson,** 21 (left), © **John Mitchell,** 23 (bottom right);
© **Karl Weidmann,** 25 (left); © **Jean-Mari Jro,** 66 (left), 68
(left); © **Wouterloot-Gregoire,** 72 (bottom insert)
Visuals Unlimited: © **William J. Weber,** 11; © **John B.
Nelson,** 19; © **Kjell B. Sandved,** 25 (right), 26 (right)
Len W. Meents: Maps on 74, 78, 83
**Courtesy Flag Research Center, Winchester,
Massachusetts 01890:** Flag on back cover
Cover: Street in Cayenne
Cover Inset: Space Center in Kourou

Motorcycles as well as cars are used for transportation in Cayenne.

TABLE OF CONTENTS

Chapter 1

LA GUYANE

French Guiana lies on the north coast of South America, facing the Atlantic Ocean. To the east and south it shares borders with Brazil, and in the west with the Republic of Suriname. To the west of Suriname is the Republic of Guyana, and these two territories together with French Guiana were for many years known as the Guianas. Until they gained independence, Guyana was a colony of Great Britain and Suriname was a Dutch colony. French Guiana was a colony of France until 1946, when it officially became *La Guyane,* an overseas department of the Republic of France with economic and political status similar to that of any department (administrative district) in France.

In South America only the Guianas were not conquered by the Spaniards or Portuguese. In the sixteenth and seventeenth centuries, many Europeans believed the Guianas were the land of the legendary *El Dorado,* a "golden kingdom." Some came to seek their fortunes. But there was little to attract settlers, and the Spaniards and Portuguese found greater treasures elsewhere.

With dense forests, countless rivers, and hostile mountains, the region was difficult to explore. Even so, by the mid-seventeenth century, a trading post had been founded on the coast at Cayenne. During the eighteenth and nineteenth centuries African slaves were imported to work on cotton and sugar plantations.

Opposite page: Low clouds touch the treetops in the rain forest.

A view of Devil's Island from Royale Island

Today the majority of French Guiana's population lives in Cayenne, the largest town, and along the coast. Most of the country is covered by tropical forest, inhabited by a small population of native Indians and some descendants of African slaves. French Guiana is approximately one-sixth the size of France, yet in 1990 the total population was only 115,000.

French Guiana is best known to the outside world for two reasons. For many years it was a penal colony where convicts and political prisoners from France and French territories were sent to serve sentences in terrible conditions, most notably on Devil's Island. More recently Kourou on the coast has been developed as the Guianese Space Center (*Center Spatial Guyanese*), or Europe's Spaceport, from which commercial Ariane rockets and satellites are launched. "The independence of France and Europe depends on Kourou," declared France's then-Premier Jacques Chirac during a visit in April 1987. There are many, however, who resent the existence of this example of European modern technology in their country, which is as yet largely undeveloped.

Chapter 2

AN UNTOUCHED LAND

French Guiana is about half the size of the state of Oklahoma. More than 90 percent of the country is covered by tropical forest, very little of which has been disturbed. It represents one of the world's few remaining areas where an extraordinary variety of plants and animals have survived in their original state. Development has taken place only in the coastal area, where Cayenne and the main towns of Kourou and Saint-Laurent du Maroni are found. But even this coastal zone remains surrounded by mangrove swamps, open savanna grasslands, and swamps rich with birds and reptiles.

The name *Guiana* is believed to come from an Indian word meaning "land of waters." There are many rivers. Two of the longest form natural borders with Suriname and, in the east, with Brazil. At least five major rivers and many small ones flow the length of the country into the Atlantic Ocean. Most have their source in the Tumuc-Humac Mountains and other low hilly ranges that form the southern border with Brazil. The rocky foundations of the land, an ancient geologic formation known as the Guiana Highlands, have undergone erosion for millions of years, so there are no significant mountain peaks in French Guiana.

The Atlantic Ocean coastline

THE COAST

The coast extends the full breadth of the country along the Atlantic Ocean for about 200 miles (about 322 kilometers), from the mouth of the Oyapock River on the Brazilian border to the mouth of the Maroni River on the Suriname border. Much of the coastal land is low and swampy with forests of mangrove trees, usually growing in thick mud or slime. In such places as near Cayenne or at Les Roches close to Kourou, low hills and rocks from the ancient Guiana Highlands reach the sea. Offshore there are a few rocky islands, most notably the Iles du Salut about 7 miles (11 kilometers) north of Kourou. Sandy beaches are rare on the coast and usually are found between the rocky points or in the northern sector near Les Hattes.

Mangrove trees thrive in the salty ocean water.

The coastline is changing constantly. Particles of sediment carried by water from the Amazon and other rivers are deposited and form mud banks that can be as much as 25 miles (40 kilometers) long. These muddy banks tend to move northwest with the general ocean current. As the banks move and grow larger, they are colonized by the rapidly growing mangroves, which become established and form a new coastline. In one place near Kourou the mangroves advanced 1.5 miles (2.4 kilometers) in the ten years between 1976 and 1986. The growth of the mangroves in some places is a nuisance. At Cayenne mangroves that reach to within a few yards of the town are being cut back.

Behind the immediate line of the coast the land rises slightly to a plain that extends inland for as much as fifty miles (eighty kilometers). This high plain is where most of the population lives. The land near Saint-Laurent du Maroni has better soils. Some areas close to the nearby town of Mana have been developed for agriculture.

Many of the plants in the forests of French Guiana also are common to the Amazon forests.

THE FORESTS

It is difficult to escape tropical vegetation in French Guiana. The forest begins on the outskirts of Cayenne. Giant trees, some reaching to heights of 120 feet (37 meters) and sometimes more, are surrounded by a profusion of plant species. It is a superb rain forest that extends unbroken, except for rivers and a few swamps, to the Tumuc-Humac Mountains in the south.

French Guiana's immense forest resembles a giant nature reserve, but the timber industry is an important part of the economy. Logging is confined to small areas less than fifty miles (eighty kilometers) from the coast, largely for practical reasons but also with an eye to guarding stocks for the future. The trees are often species that are common in Amazon forests, though, as

*Vines cover the trees in a swamp forest (left) and yellow flowers
bloom on the tabebuias tree in the tropical rain forest (right).*

usual in such large areas, there are different percentages of each
species according to soil, drainage, and position on hillsides. The
local names for the trees often are French. *Ébène verte,* the
tabebuias tree, is a yellow flowering species with an extremely
hard wood, and *fromager,* the ceiba tree, produces an abundance of
kapok, rather like cotton wool, around its seeds. Other trees are
named from forest Indian languages: *wacapou,* a fine tree, is
common throughout the forests of the Guianas and the
northwestern Amazon. Another, the *yayamadou,* is the local species
of a type of tree found bordering swampy places in all the
Amazon tropical forests.

Palms of many kinds are common, some within the forest itself,
some forming their own special forests, and others typically seen
in the savannas and swamps. They have been useful to the South
American Indians for generations because they are a valuable
source of oils, hard wood, leaves for thatch, and fibers for many
uses.

The Swamp of Kaw

SWAMPS AND SAVANNAS

The largest swamp, the *Marais de Kaw,* literally "The Swamp of Kaw," covers about 250,000 acres (about 101,000 hectares) between the Mahury and Approuague Rivers to the southeast of Cayenne. This wilderness of swamp vegetation, palms, and mangroves is traversed by numerous creeks. It is bounded in the south by low hills, the Mountains of Kaw, which are covered with thick, tropical rain forest.

As a wilderness the swamp is exceptional, particularly as there are few people in the area to intrude. The principal danger is from "weekenders" from Cayenne or Kourou with their high-powered speedboats. Local environmentalists are pressing for part of the swamp to be designated a zone of special ecological interest. The vast swamp is clearly an important wetland and as

Savannas stretch along the coast.

such has become high on the international agenda for protection. Other extensive swamps border some parts of the rivers even far inland and are noted for their wildlife, particularly reptiles and birds.

Along the coast there are large areas of open grassland or savannas. The vegetation is not lush, but some savanna plants can be colorful, such as the purple gentians or small red heliconias. Occasionally the savannas, especially those near Mana, are studded with groups of palms, making small forest "islands" that provide cover for many birds and small mammals.

RIVERS

The rivers that rise in the southern mountains are fed by the high rainfall and develop quickly as they flow up to 250 miles or

The Maroni River becomes wider as it nears the sea.

so (about 400 kilometers) to empty into the Atlantic Ocean. The longest, the Maroni River, rises in the Tumuc-Humac range. For the upper part of its course it is known as the Litani River; then in midcourse the name changes to Lawa. It eventually becomes the Maroni for about the last 100 miles (161 kilometers) to the sea, by which time it is about 2 miles (3.2 kilometers) wide. The second-largest river is the Oyapock, which forms the border with Brazil. Other rivers include the Mana, which begins near Saul, a small settlement in the central highlands, and the Sinnamary, which begins on the other side of a divide only a short distance away.

All the rivers of French Guiana have courses that descend from the highlands in a series of *sauts,* low waterfalls or rapids, around which the local boatmen drag the canoes they call *pirogues.* On important routes the early pioneers built narrow-gauge rail track that is now in a state of disrepair. Along these tracks wagons were pushed by hand to transport goods around the falls. In their lower courses, immediately inland from the coast, the rivers offer easier access, and some of the rivers are navigable by small boats up to sixty miles (ninety-six kilometers) from the mouth.

Occasionally the sauts may be several feet high and present a considerable obstacle to navigation. The Sauts Machicou and Canori on the Approuague River are impressive, with a drop of nineteen feet (six meters) in three hundred feet (ninety-one meters) of rapids. At Petit Saut, one of the falls on the Sinnamary River, a low dam is being built to create a lake and a hydroelectric generating plant.

THE CLIMATE

Because French Guiana is near the equator, the daytime temperature is almost constantly high, averaging 79 degrees Fahrenheit (26 degrees Celsius), with little variation between seasons or day and night. In the forest interior the nights can be noticeably cooler especially in the few hours before dawn.

The rainfall is heavy. There is a distinct "dry" season of about four months beginning in July and a shorter, drier week or two that precedes the rainy season. The wettest time is in May when in Cayenne the rainfall is more than eleven times greater than in September, the driest month. In Cayenne the annual rainfall totals about 120 inches (about 300 centimeters) per year. In Kaw the rainfall is higher, totaling about 150 inches (about 380 centimeters). Some parts of the country are drier. Around Mana the rainfall is less than 77 inches (196 centimeters) per year, which together with good soils makes the region better for agriculture.

Tropical blossoms include bluish-violet flowers of the jacaranda trees (left) and colorful orchids (above).

FLORA

With a tropical climate and a variety of environments, the plants of French Guiana have an immense diversity. Most obvious is the profusion of tropical blossoms. The forest has many bright flowering trees including the tabebuias; the jacarandas, locally called *copaya*, with their masses of bluish-violet flowers; and the qualeas typical of the Guianas with whitish-pink, or sometimes purple, flowers. Within the forest and crowning it are the vines, or lianas, and epiphytes, plants that find a foothold on the trees. Orchids with delicate flowers are numerous, and so are the philodendrons with their large glossy leaves. Bromeliads, from the family found throughout the Americas, frequently have brilliant flowers. Also in the forest are bright heliconias, of the same family as bananas, and colorful *Strelitzia*, or bird of paradise

Water hyacinths (above) and a bird of paradise (inset)

flowers. Some of the forest plants, such as the red annatto and the purple genipa, with which the Indians paint their bodies, are used commercially as dyes.

The rocky sauts of some rivers are covered with plants that live partly in water and raise flowers above the surface. In the lower courses where the water is still and in the swamps, purple-flowered water hyacinths, in French the *jacinthe d'eau*, cover the surface.

FAUNA

The wildlife is typical of the tropical Americas. Many species are well known in the United States, particularly in the southern states. Among familiar animals are the common opossum, the cougar, skunks, and armadillos. Less familiar are the many species

Capuchin monkeys (above) and a tapir (right)

of South American primates: the monkeys and marmosets. Some of these are frequently seen crossing the tarmac roads that have been laid through the rain forest. Among the largest monkeys are the howlers, which roam the forest in groups of about fifteen individuals and can be heard a mile or more away, making a noise like roaring wind. Spider monkeys and capuchin monkeys, also frequently seen in the forest, often are caught and kept as pets by the country people. The monkeys, like some of the other South American mammals, have prehensile tails that can be used for grasping, just like a hand, or for balance as the monkeys scramble along the branches.

The forest floor animals include small deer about 2 feet (60 centimeters) high, which are perfectly colored so they merge with the background. Giant otters, some measuring almost 7 feet (2 meters) from their nose to the tip of the tail, live in the rivers. The largest mammal is the tapir, a hoofed, tailless, short-legged

A jaguarundi (above) and an anteater (right)

beast that can weigh up to 400 pounds (181 kilograms). Tapirs browse the lush foliage using a short but flexible snout.

Many of the mammals, including monkeys and tapirs, are traditional game hunted by the Indians and other forest dwellers. The semiaquatic capybaras, the pacas, and the agoutis are all rodents that are considered delicacies. So too is the peccary or wild pig. The meat of these animals is sold in the markets. These forest floor mammals are also the natural prey of the carnivores, which include jaguars, ocelots, jaguarundi, and the margay, all species of wild cats.

Some of the curiosities of the forest are the anteaters and sloths, members of a unique South American group of animals. The tamandua, locally known as the *tamanoi* and prominent in Indian folklore, is an anteater with a prehensile tail that climbs trees in search of termite nests. Sloths, or *parsou-mouton,* spend their lives in the trees, especially in the spindly cecropias, moving slowly from place to place while browsing on leaves. The sloth's shaggy coat is often tinged green with tiny algae, which provide excellent camouflage. Among the many animals in this tropical country it is hard to miss the insects. Butterflies abound, particularly the giant morphos with their iridescent blue wings. There are giant beetles and spiders that are sometimes ten inches (twenty-five centimeters) across.

Reptiles of the swamps and rivers include the caiman, the South American crocodilian, with some large specimens up to seven feet (two meters) long, and occasionally longer if they have not been disturbed. Snakes too are found in the swamps, including anacondas, perhaps the bulkiest if not the longest of the world's snakes. In drier places there are rattlesnakes and the highly venomous fer-de-lance, as well as brightly colored coral snakes, including the false coral. Certain species of snakes are extremely difficult to see. Some are as thin as shoelaces and resemble the small vines they use for concealment. Others are brilliant green, like the color of young branches.

Often a rustle in the dry leaves on the forest floor or beside a track does not mean a snake but the rapid movement of one of several kinds of iguana lizards. Some are small, brilliantly colored green and rust. The largest live in trees and rocky places and reach a length of 2 or 3 feet (0.6 or 0.9 meter). Such lizards are harmless and sought for their flesh or eggs, another local delicacy.

Perhaps one of the most remarkable gatherings of any animal in French Guiana is the annual return of the marine turtles, including the giant leatherbacks, to the sandy beaches at Les Hattes near the mouth of the Maroni River, where they lay their eggs. For three or four months, beginning in April, several species of turtles emerge from the sea and struggle up the gently sloping

Anacondas (left) are well camouflaged. The three-toed sloth (above) and a green iguana (below) also live in the forests of French Guiana.

Scarlet ibis live amid the mangrove roots.
A marine turtle lays eggs on the beach (inset).

beach. Over the period of the nesting season many thousands of turtles lay eggs before returning to the sea, and though protection there is minimal, the animals are monitored by the forestry service and the World Wide Fund for Nature.

BIRDS

French Guiana with its variety of tropical habitats is home to many bird species. Large colonies of seabirds are found on small islands of Le Grande Connetable and Le Petit Connetable, only twenty-five miles (forty kilometers) from Cayenne. In the early part of the twentieth century their guano was collected by an American company. Today the islets are set aside as reserves. The mangroves, especially northwest of Kourou, are visited by tourists to see the many scarlet ibis. At one time there were thousands of these brilliantly colored birds, but a trade in their feathers has

Hoatzins (above) and colorful macaws (right)

seriously depleted their numbers. When the tide is low groups of ibis search the exposed mud banks for small crustaceans, worms, and insects. If disturbed they take flight to the mangroves.

The forest and riversides are home to many bird species, but it is often easier to hear them than to see them. The forest sounds include the raucous screeching calls of macaws and parrots of many kinds, the melodic call of tinamous, or the metallic call of bellbirds that sounds like a gong. Woodpeckers drum their bills against dead trees, and tiny hummingbirds set the air vibrating with their rapid wing beats. Living in marshy places and along the rivers are egrets and herons, including the curious boat-billed heron. The American Wood stork, the Maguari stork, and the tall Jabiru stork can be seen occasionally, as can the unusual hoatzin, a bird that can hardly fly.

Among the largest of the birds are the harpy eagles that live high in the forest canopy, where they prey on small monkeys and

*Both the harpy eagle (above) and piranha fish (right)
are dangerous to other animals.*

other treetop mammals or lizards. Vultures too are numerous,
with the black-headed vulture commonly seen around the edge of
villages. The more colorful and larger king vulture is a bird of the
forests.

FISH

The rivers, estuaries, and sea contain an abundance of fish of
many species that form the basis for much of the country-style
food. The piranha, the so-called cannibal fish, is voracious and has
razor-sharp teeth. Though always noted as "full of bones," the
piranha is excellent for eating and regarded by some Indians as a
delicacy. Other good food fish are the pacu and the coumarou, a
fish that feeds on the fleshy leaves of some water plants. Small

sharks, red snapper, and crustaceans, such as the large shrimp locally known as *crevette*, provide the basis of the country's small fishing industry and are widely used in local dishes.

In addition to the piranha, three other fish have bad reputations. The aimara or naima may grow to about 3 feet (0.9 meter) and has needle-sharp teeth. The electric eel is a long, rather heavy-bodied fish that has specially modified muscles that produce electricity. Any animal unfortunate enough to be in the water nearby can receive a shock ranging from a mild tingle to a charge that can be fatal. The ray, a flattened triangular-shaped fish, has a venomous spine on its back. An unwary bather who steps on a ray can receive an excruciatingly painful wound that soon becomes gangrenous.

NATURAL RESOURCES

Apart from its immense tropical forest and its rivers, French Guiana has few natural resources. Small deposits of gold, bauxite, and kaolin are known, but exploitation has not proved to be economic. Agriculture is also limited by the lack of good soils and, in places, by excessive rainfall.

The forest, on the other hand, provides many high-value natural products. Its greatest resource is the variety of timber, especially tropical hardwoods, that could be of considerable value to the world's furniture and construction industries. There are major problems, however, in exploiting the timber, not least the need for access to the forest by good roads. Creating this infrastructure has to date proved both difficult and costly. French Guiana's other important resource is its many rivers, which are well suited to the production of hydroelectric energy.

The ruins of the walls of the prison on Devil's Island

POTENTIAL

For most of its history, French Guiana has been a colony with a limited economy based on sugar plantations and slave labor. When that was no longer possible, it became a penal colony and remained so for one hundred years. During that time, almost nothing was done to develop agriculture, transport, or the economy. The population remained small, and as a country it gained a bad reputation as a place to which convicts were sent. Only in the last half of the twentieth century has French Guiana been able to consider how it might develop its potential and how it might become less dependent on aid from France. The development of Kourou and the Guianese Space Center has made an important contribution, but now French Guiana has to determine how it can best develop its own resources.

Alonso de Ojeda (far left) and Amerigo Vespucci (left)

Chapter 3

EXPLORATION AND SETTLEMENT

THE WILD COAST

Following in the footsteps of Christopher Columbus, a number of explorers set out from Europe at the beginning of the sixteenth century hoping to find a route to India. Like Columbus, several reached the South American mainland. In 1500, the Spaniard Vicente Yáñez Pinzón was probably the first European to note the fresh muddy water at the mouths of the continent's two most famous rivers: the Amazon and the Orinoco. In the same year an expedition led by two other explorers, Alonso de Ojeda and Amerigo Vespucci, was the first to make landfall on the coast of present-day French Guiana.

The region that became known as the "Guiana coast" extends between the mouths of the Orinoco and Amazon Rivers, a distance of some 1,000 miles (1,609 kilometers). As Vespucci observed, it is a land of mud and mangroves. The early explorers found it difficult to penetrate and gave it the name of the "Wild Coast." After a short time they virtually abandoned the region in favor of the Venezuelan coast farther north, where they found pearls, and Colombia in the west, where gold was plentiful in the coastal rivers.

Within a few years, the Spaniards, spurred on by the promise of even more gold, had conquered the two great civilizations of ancient America: the Aztecs in Mexico and the Incas in Peru. The Viceroyalty of Peru, governed from Spain, was established in 1543. Great quantities of silver were mined by Indians working in slave conditions. In 1545-1546 Francisco de Orellana, who was searching for rare spices in the uncharted Amazonian forests, became the first European to descend the Amazon River. By contrast the Wild Coast of Guiana was all but forgotten for most of the sixteenth century except by a few adventurers trading Indian slaves and brazilwood, a very hard wood that yields a valuable red dye.

SEARCH FOR EL DORADO

In their search for gold the Spaniards learned from the native Indians of the legendary kingdom of El Dorado hidden among mountains far in the interior. Many expeditions were organized and performed remarkable feats of exploration. Rumor eventually led explorers into the region of the Orinoco River and the Guianas. There a mythical lake called Manoa became part of the El Dorado legend.

The first, and in many ways most courageous, expeditions were made by the Spaniard Antonio de Berrío. He had been told by tribes of Indians that "he must seek rich lands in the hills of Guiana beyond the Orinoco." The "Guiana" referred to at that

A woodcut showing Antonio de Berrío, captured by the English

time also included the south of present-day Venezuela, an area now known as the Guayana highlands. The problem facing Berrío was to find a way through the high and inhospitable mountains that separate the Guianas from the *llanos,* or grasslands, of the Orinoco River. Despite many setbacks, including the loss of many of his men, illness, treachery, rains, and desertion, Berrío continued with his quest but was unsuccessful.

News of the Spanish explorations had reached England, and some prominent English sailors decided to try their luck. In 1595 Sir Robert Dudley was the first Englishman to send a crew up the Orinoco. Later in the same year, Sir Walter Raleigh arrived. He took Berrío prisoner, learned all he could about Manoa, and set off up the Orinoco River. Although he spent barely a month upriver, he saw enough of the beautiful landscape and rivers and heard so much about gold that he determined to return. Back in

Sir Walter Raleigh

England Raleigh wrote the first book on the region, his famous *Discoverie of the large, rich and beautiful Empire of Guiana, with a relation of the great and golden citie of Manoa (which the Spaniards call El Dorado).*

In January 1596 Lawrence Keymis, who accompanied Raleigh on his first expedition, was dispatched with orders to explore all the rivers north of the mouth of the Amazon. He surveyed the whole of the coast between the Amazon and the Orinoco. He made a systematic record of all the rivers, the tribes and their languages, and the products of the region. Keymis encountered more rumors of gold and mines, but not El Dorado. In the same year, another of Raleigh's lieutenants, Leonard Berry, was sent to explore the rivers of the Guianas.

Meanwhile Raleigh had fallen into disfavor with Queen Elizabeth I and was imprisoned in the Tower of London. It was not until his release in 1616 that Raleigh could return to search for El Dorado. He was then in his sixties and not in the best of health. But he organized a splendid expedition that included Keymis, Raleigh's son Wat, and his nephew George. The fleet reached the Cayenne River in November, and the mouth of the Orinoco in December. Raleigh was not fit to undertake the journey upriver, so he dispatched Keymis, with Wat, 250 soldiers, and 150 sailors and sent them off in 5 vessels. The expedition was a total failure. Keymis could not locate the gold mines he had been told of on his previous journey and later committed suicide. Wat was killed in an attack on the Spanish garrison town of San Tomé near the Orinoco mouth. Raleigh was forced to end a brilliant career by returning to England a failure. He was executed the following year.

THE COLONISTS

During the years when Raleigh was a prisoner in the Tower of London his book was widely studied in Europe. It became clear to several governments that no settlements had yet been made in the Guiana region. Inevitably a few colonial powers were tempted to try.

The Dutch were already trading in salt with people of what is now the Venezuelan coast. In 1597-1598 the first recorded Dutch expedition arrived on the Guiana coast. It followed in the tracks of Raleigh and Keymis, exploring the shoreline and many of the rivers, and successfully trading with the Indians. In 1602 Henri IV of France gave permission for the creation of a Guiana colony. The first serious French reconnaissance took place in 1604 led by the nobleman Daniel de la Ravardière and his associate Moquet. The first efforts of the English to establish a colony were

The Oyapock River

concentrated on the Oyapock River, by Sir John and Charles Leigh, friends of Raleigh, between 1602 and 1606, and three years later by Robert Harcourt from Stanton Harcourt, a village near Oxford, England. Harcourt's aim was to start a peaceful farming colony, but the dream of Manoa was never far from his mind. Two years after Harcourt, Sir Thomas Roe made an extensive investigation of the same area, starting at the Amazon and working his way north.

None of these earliest attempts to settle succeeded. It was not until 1616 that the beginning of a permanent settlement took place. In that year a private company of Zeeland merchants from Holland established a trading post on the Essequibo River (in present-day Guyana). After the first five years it was supported by the Dutch West India Company, created in 1621. For many years the company regularly sent vessels with a supply of articles for bartering with the native Indians. In exchange for axes, knives, cloth, beads, and scissors, the vessels returned with the red annatto dye and tobacco. The Dutch had an advantage over their European rivals because Dutch knowledge and experience of their own flat, watery country equipped them better to face the swampy conditions of the coastlands of the Guianas.

Despite several expeditions, the French initially were not successful in their colonization attempts. In 1626, 1630, and 1633 small colonies of twenty-five, fifty, and sixty people attempted to settle near the coast. In 1643 a commercial company called the Cape North Company was formed in Rouen. A group of some three hundred people arrived, led by one of the company's associates, Poncet de Brétigny, a wealthy gentleman from Normandy. They settled in present-day Cayenne around Cépérou Hill, which they named after the Indian chief who lived there. Brétigny assumed the title of governor and lieutenant-general for the king, but Brétigny was a vain, cruel man, quite unsuited to the task. He created hostility not only among his own people but also, and especially, among the native Indians. He was murdered a year later by the Galibi Indians who lived on the coast, and many of the colonists suffered a similar fate. A few of the settlers managed to escape west into land held by the Dutch, but the Indians continued to take reprisals against the small groups of colonists who were left behind.

Another company, formed in 1652, sent between seven hundred and eight hundred people from Le Havre, on the north coast of France, to Cayenne. That settlement too failed because of disease, internal rivalry, and hostility from the Indians.

The Dutch then took over the area around Cayenne. In 1664 some two hundred French colonists arrived from La Rochelle. The Dutch fled from Cayenne without a fight, giving the newly

King Louis XIV of France

arrived colonists the opportunity to settle under the gifted leadership of Antoine Lefébure de la Barre. A diplomatic and conciliatory man, de la Barre secured the goodwill of the Indians and laid the foundations of the first permanent French settlement.

During its first years the settlement was troubled by the upheaval from wars between European powers, principally the English and the Dutch. The French colony at Cayenne surrendered to the English Admiral Harmon in 1667. In the same year the territory was returned to France in the Treaty of Breda, which marked the end of the second Anglo-Dutch War. In 1676 the colony fell into the hands of the Dutch, and King Louis XIV of France ordered that Cayenne be retaken. A fleet was dispatched from Brest under the command of Admiral J. d'Estrées, who regained the town. After the victorious peace treaty of Nimeque in 1678, Louis XIV ordered that a special medal be struck. It bore the words *Cayana Recuperata,* "Cayenne Recovered."

THE SLAVES

Toward the end of the seventeenth century agricultural development began in the colony. Coffee, cocoa, vanilla, cotton, and sugarcane were cultivated. In the eighteenth century the colony became important as a producer of cotton and the world's major supplier of the red annatto dye. The Indians, however, were unsuited to work on farms or plantations. Instead the Guianas became dependent for labor on black slaves imported from Africa.

Black slaves taken from Africa had first been introduced to the region by the Englishman Lord Willoughby. In 1650 he took possession of the area that is now Suriname and claimed it for England. Between 1651 and 1667, with the labor of some thirty thousand slaves, about five hundred plantations were established in the region run by British and French colonizers. The French created the Company of the Guyane for slave traffic, but it often preferred to sell its cargo of blacks to the Caribbean island of Saint Domingue (present-day Haiti). Even so, in just over sixty years between 1677 and 1740, the black population in the French-held territory increased from one thousand to almost five thousand, and toward the end of the seventeenth century, to ten thousand. This was, though, a relatively small number, compared with the eighty thousand slaves in the neighboring Dutch territory.

Slavery in the colonies was governed by the harsh *code noir,* "black code," issued in 1685. Slaves were chattels and not allowed any rights to property or any personal protection. Punishment was left to the discretion of their masters, who were usually ruthless. The slaves could not enter any form of contract. Some had to have their master's permission to marry. Only in one aspect did

An engraving of a Maroon village in the 1860s

the code noir hold out any hope. It was an established principle from the beginning that some slaves should be permitted to buy or gain their freedom. Additionally, it was decreed that any slave who was freed by his master was entitled to the full legal rights of citizenship.

In both French and Dutch territories, the blacks easily outnumbered the whites. In the Dutch territory many escaped, fleeing into the forest. In the late seventeenth and eighteenth centuries local slave rebellions resulted, on more than one occasion, in the escape of an entire labor force from a plantation. So large were their numbers that the escapees were able to establish themselves in independent self-governing communities. In time the authorities could do nothing but accept the situation, and "peace treaties" were signed freeing the slaves, who remained in the interior. They became known as *marrons*, or "wild" slaves; in English they were called "Maroons."

THE KOUROU EXPEDITION

Compared with their British and Dutch neighbors, the French in Guiana were making very slow progress. By the 1760s their cultivated plantation territory was limited to the area around Cayenne and a few places along the coast.

Some degree of order had been achieved by the religious missionaries, the Jesuits, who arrived to convert as many people as possible to Catholicism. As elsewhere in South America, the Jesuits created missions and took hundreds of Indians under their protection. The missionaries gave the Indians some basic education and taught them how to cultivate crops. In return the Indians provided the missionaries with a workforce. The system benefited both peoples, and there was considerable disruption when the Jesuits were expelled from the territory in 1762.

In 1763 the Seven Years' War between England and France ended, with the disastrous loss for France of colonies in North America, several Caribbean islands, and most notably its largest colony, Canada. As if to compensate for this loss, and in response to the regular complaints of administrators in Guiana that they lacked manual labor, Louis XV's minister, Choiseul, decided to send a large expedition of fourteen thousand people to the colony without any preparations and with no regard as to the lack of facilities there. These unfortunates, mostly from the Lorraine area, were persuaded to make the journey with the lure of "a land of promise with an ideal climate for cultivating plantations." They had no idea of the real conditions that awaited them.

The expedition was a total disaster. Arriving on the beaches of Kourou at the beginning of the rainy season, without even the most basic necessities of food and shelter, most of the people soon succumbed to tropical diseases. On June 9, 1765, M. de Chanvalon, who had been appointed administrator of the New Colony, reported that ten thousand had died. Others fled to the islands off the coast, including Devil's Island, an act, it is claimed, from which the islands took their name of *Iles du Salut,* or "Islands of Salvation." Some two thousand of the original expedition made their way back to France.

PEACE, PROSPERITY, AND THE PORTUGUESE

Toward the end of the eighteenth century, the fortunes of the French started to change for the better, largely due to the efforts of Victor Malouet, the governor who arrived in the colony in 1776. He secured the help of an engineer, Jean-Samuel Guisan, who was working for the Dutch in Guiana and appointed him administrator of rural affairs and director of works in the French territory. Guisan surveyed the land and introduced reforms. Instead of cultivating high ground that drains quickly, crops were transferred to the wet, fertile lowlands, where drainage and canalization were introduced to dry out the swamps. In a relatively short time Guisan transformed the agricultural economy. A few years of prosperity followed.

These good years were short-lived, however, as repercussions of the French Revolution of 1789 spread to the overseas colony. In 1793 Jeannet-Oudin, a nephew of Danton, one of the leaders of the revolution, arrived in Cayenne with a decree abolishing slavery. The effect on the colony was devastating, because although the number of slaves was still relatively small, most were employed on the plantations, which were the basis of the economy. At the same time a number of deportees, many of them political prisoners whose "crimes" were connected with the French Revolution, were sent from France to Cayenne in the vain hope that they might help develop the territory. Many of them died. Nonetheless, it was the first step in the establishment of the territory as a penal colony or a place of exile.

From 1800 to 1809 the territory was governed by Victor Hugues, a military man who had served in Guadeloupe, a French island in the Caribbean. His instructions were to bring back order and restart the economy. In 1802 the French authorities permitted the reintroduction of slavery. Former slaves living close to the plantations were brought back without too much difficulty. But it was virtually impossible to entice back those who had established agricultural communities along the rivers and in the forest.

After 1803 the British navy launched a massive attack on French colonial possessions throughout the Caribbean and elsewhere. The British helped the Portuguese from Brazil to seize Cayenne. The Portuguese were retaliating against Napoleon's invasion of Portugal in 1807. Cayenne remained in their hands from 1809 to 1817. The Portuguese compared the state of the French colony with their own land around Pará (in present-day Brazil), and soon recognized the negligence of the French authorities. In particular they noted the poor state of the economy and the lack of communication. The Portuguese occupation gave the French territory access to Brazil's markets, encouraged overseas trade, and reinforced slavery, which the Portuguese believed was essential to get the most from the plantations. These were quite prosperous years, but little was done to make fundamental changes that might have helped the colony. In 1814, following the defeat of Napoleon Bonaparte in Europe, Cayenne finally was returned to France, although the Portuguese remained until 1817.

Chapter 4

GOLD, CONVICTS, AND COLONIAL RULE

MOTHER JAVOUHEY

The code noir, the document on which slavery was based, had always allowed for a certain number of slaves to go free. In time this created a "free colored class" who, although technically free to do what they wished, only survived with difficulty. The whites did not accept them, and as freed slaves they had no trade on which to rebuild their lives. This predicament was recognized by Mother Superior Anne-Marie Javouhey, one of the "saints" of French Guiana, a person whose name is still revered more than a hundred years after her death.

Mother Javouhey of the community of St. Joseph of Cluny arrived in French Guiana in 1827 with a few sisters of the religious order. She founded a pioneering mission on the shore of the Mana River at a spot known as Terre-Rouge, which later became the town of Mana. The government gave her a small subsidy, but she used her own money to buy a few slaves to help build the mission. She cultivated the land around the mission and encouraged the slaves to plant sugarcane, coffee, bananas, and manioc. It was far enough upriver not to be influenced by the political corruption of Cayenne. Within a few years the mission was flourishing.

In the late eighteenth century the abolition of slavery had become a worldwide issue. It was inevitable that it would come about in French Guiana as elsewhere. During the 1830s Mother Javouhey took charge of some five hundred slaves who were to be freed. To help raise funds for her mission, she founded a rum distillery at Mana, using the sugarcane from her own plantations. The distillery prospered, and the reputation of the rum lasted long after the distillery closed.

She also counted lepers among her friends. In 1833, hearing of the desperate condition of one group on the Iles du Salut, she decided to visit them. What she found appalled her: eighty men and women living in the most miserable conditions, uncared for, ignored by the authorities, and in urgent need of medical and practical help. She persuaded the governor to put the group into her care, and the lepers were transferred to a settlement near Mana. There, in a sheltered place with fresh running water, she organized the building of a leper hospital. She arranged regular visits by a doctor, a chaplain, and two of the sisters from the convent.

But in time the government ceased to support her. She acquired enemies, particularly among the *Creoles* (native-born persons with some European blood) who owned plantations and who believed Mother Javouhey was depriving them of slaves. An attempt to murder her on one of her visits upriver to the hospital failed when the boatman charged with this task lost his nerve. She left

A display of machinery used on sugar plantations in the nineteenth century

the colony, an elderly lady, two years before slavery was officially and finally abolished on May 1, 1848. Back in Europe it is said that she often wept for the great forests of Mana and "her black children."

ABOLITION OF SLAVERY

At the time of abolition, there were 19,000 slaves in French Guiana, 4,000 free "colored" (former slaves), and 1,200 whites. In 1840 only 3,500 slaves were working on twenty-nine sugar plantations, most of which had steam-driven mills, and the effect on the economy was devastating. Sugar production dropped from about 5 million pounds (more than 2 million kilograms) in 1847 to about 885,000 pounds (about 400,000 kilograms) in 1851. The combined effect of the abolition of slavery and the development of the sugar beet in France meant that by 1880, most plantations were finished, abandoned to the forest.

Some plantations, however, managed to continue producing some sugar, and also cotton, pimento, and annatto dye. But many former slaves preferred to take up subsistence farming, growing only enough food for their own needs. As a result there was a serious shortfall in manpower, and the colony faced a severe financial crisis. To fill the labor gap, the colony turned to Asia, as British and Dutch Guiana also had done. But French Guiana was much less successful than its neighbors in attracting immigrants. The story goes that the first Indian-hired laborers to arrive were, in a sense, hijacked. They were in a three-masted boat on its way to the French Caribbean island of Guadeloupe, when the ship hit a submerged rock off the French Guiana coast. The date was June 2, 1856. The ship called in for repairs and the passengers were put ashore. The governor at the time, Admiral Beaudin, took advantage of this piece of luck and persuaded some of the new arrivals to stay and work in French Guiana.

GOLD FEVER

No doubt the newcomers were influenced to stay by the news that the first gold strike in French Guiana had been made a few years earlier. A Brazilian hunter called Paolino made the discovery in the Arataye River, a tributary of the Approuague. Hundreds of people—former slaves, foreigners, and whites—left Cayenne and made their way deep into the forest following the gold trail. In 1857 four Guianese created the *Company Aurifère et Agricole de l'Approuague* (The Gold and Agricultural Company of the River Approuague).

More discoveries followed between 1873 and 1878 in the region of Saint-Elie, largely owing to the efforts of a Guianese prospector,

M.T. Vitalo, who made huge profits from the finds. Spurred on by his success, Vitalo moved into the area of the then-disputed Dutch-French border, unleashing a gold rush of some six thousand people who followed him. Another gold discovery by two prospectors in the Carsevene River was also in a disputed zone. The boundary between French Guiana and Brazil had never been settled, and the ownership of the large region of Amapa immediately north of the Amazon mouth was unresolved. The matter of the disputed frontiers was put to arbitration, with Russia and Switzerland deciding to whom the land belonged. In each case French Guiana was the loser.

The last gold rush occurred in 1901 in the interior of the country, in the Inini and Haute-Mana regions. And with it died the hopes of great fortunes. In reality, all the gold discoveries were quite modest and did not bring prosperity to the colony. Indeed they had an adverse effect, because so many men left the plantations that the agricultural development of the country was badly damaged.

THE PENAL COLONY

Convicts had been sent to French Guiana since the end of the eighteenth century. In 1852 Emperor Napoleon III of France made the decision to send more, with a view to helping the hard-pressed colony with a supply of manpower. In effect it was an efficient way to rid France of anyone considered to be criminal, dangerous, or simply unwanted for political reasons. The first two thousand convicts arrived in 1851. Later, convicts were sent from all parts of the French Empire. In all, some seventy thousand men arrived in the colony over a period of eighty years.

Convicts were taken ashore (inset) to transportation centers and then sent on to camps in places such as Devil's Island.

Far from helping to improve conditions, the terrible level of existence endured by the prisoners only added to the bad reputation of the colony. Most convicts arrived in a notorious ship, the *Martinière,* and were first transferred to the transportation camp at Saint-Laurent du Maroni. From here the prisoners were sent to other centers. Camps existed along the coast, in the interior forest, on some remote rivers, and—most dreaded—on the Iles du Salut. The island comprises three islets. Ile Royale, the largest, consisted of 70 acres (28 hectares) and housed administration offices and hospital. The Ile Saint-Joseph, with an area of 50 acres (20 hectares), held the grim solitary confinement cells. Devil's Island itself was just 35 acres (14 hectares). Devil's Island is separated from Royale by only 240 yards (219 meters) of sea, but the currents are strong and treacherous. The island was considered escape proof. For anyone who tried his luck in the water, there was danger from sharks. In

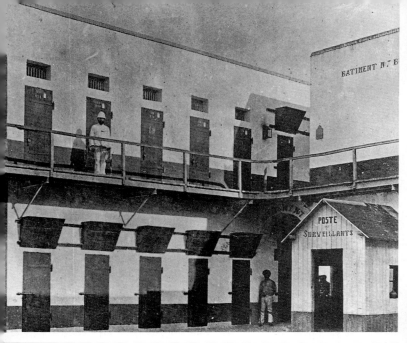

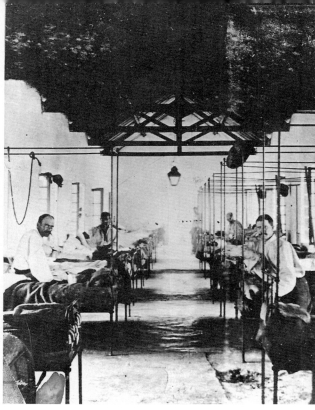

Guards were always on duty at the main detention house (above) on Devil's Island. To escape hard labor, prisoners tried to get sent to the hospital (right).

the days of the penal colony a transporter wire linked Devil's Island and Royale so that food could be passed across to the few special detainees, mostly political prisoners.

Apart from the normal deprivations of prison life—little food, primitive sanitation, and a grueling day's work in tropical conditions—prisoners faced horrendous punishment or death if they stepped out of line. Some prisoners were placed in solitary confinement for years, in tiny cells, some of which were underground, with only rats or bats for company. It is estimated that more than 10 percent of the convict population died every year, and the prisoners were refused a Christian burial. The bodies were tied in sacks and thrown into the sea to the mercy of the sharks and, if from the Iles du Salut, to the sound of the tolling of the chapel bells on the Ile Royale.

If a prisoner managed to survive his sentence, he might then face the system known as "doubling," whereby he had to serve

Left: On Royale Island, the prisoners' cells were very small.
Above: Ruins of the staff building on Devil's Island

an equal length of time in French Guiana but outside the prison camps. This meant finding work locally perhaps as a servant or gardener or in some menial job at which he earned barely enough to feed himself. Any former prisoner was at the mercy of his employer, who often took advantage of the prisoner's situation.

French Guiana as a penal colony came to an end only after the investigations of journalist Albert Londres and others in the 1930s revealed the truth. Londres's highly critical exposé persuaded the French National Assembly to vote for the penal colony's abolition in 1938, on the request of deputy G. Monnerville, a Guianese citizen. Not until 1954, however, were the last convicts returned to France. The legacy of horror, fact, and fiction is something that the people would rather forget. Some convicts, however, known today as "old whites," remained in the colony. Most stayed because they had nowhere else to go, but a few stayed because, in a strange way, they had become attached to the place that had been "home" for so many years.

Alfred Dreyfus (right) spent four years on Devil's Island for a crime he did not commit. Henri Charrière (far right) was called Papillon, "Butterfly," because of the tattoo on his chest.

CAPTAIN DREYFUS AND "PAPILLON"

The two most famous inhabitants of the Iles du Salut were Captain Alfred Dreyfus and "Papillon," the nickname of convict Henri Charrière, who wrote a best-selling book that included some of his experiences.

The case of Captain Dreyfus was a *cause cèlébre,* "celebrated case," in France at the beginning of the twentieth century. The son of a wealthy Jewish manufacturer, Dreyfus held a junior post in the French war department in 1894. He was accused of treason, a charge based on the similarity of his handwriting to that on some documents addressed to the German military attaché in Paris. On very dubious evidence he was tried, found guilty, and condemned to Devil's Island.

Fortunately for Dreyfus, an industrious friend, the chief of intelligence, Colonel Picquart, dug deeper into the matter and found evidence that a certain Major Esterhazy was the traitor. Esterhazy was tried but acquitted, and Picquart was forced to leave the army. But the case was taken up by others in France. The authorities, sensing that a plot was afoot to get Dreyfus off the island, secured him at times with chains to his bed, inside a house in total isolation. In time the scandal became a major issue that the authorities could not ignore. Dreyfus was tried again in his absence and again found guilty, but this time pardoned. Twelve years later the guilty verdict was overturned. Finally, in 1930, documents in the German military attaché's office proved without doubt that Esterhazy was guilty. Dreyfus, all the time an innocent man, had spent four miserable years on Devil's Island. He was honored throughout France as a symbol of police injustice.

Papillon also writes that he was a victim of a gross injustice, when in 1931 he was convicted for a murder he says he did not commit. Sentenced for life and deported to French Guiana in 1933, he could think of little else but escape. He made his first attempt from the hospital soon after arrival in Saint-Laurent by making off down the Maroni River with two companions in a rotten, leaky boat. After many adventures and grueling days at sea they reached the coast of Colombia, where they were captured by the local authorities.

Again Papillon managed to escape but was soon caught and sent back to the French authorities. He was confined for two years on the Iles du Salut, where he spent a year in solitary imprisonment in the medieval conditions of a small dark cell and compulsory total silence. His harrowing account is supported by other records and reports. After two years of loneliness, he again made plans to escape and eventually succeeded. His book and a feature film have forever linked French Guiana to its history as a penal colony.

Napoleon III

COLONIAL GOVERNMENT

Most people in French Guiana have had full French citizenship and the right to vote since 1848. After 1854 the colony was governed by a senate decree of Napoleon III. In 1875 all French colonies, which in the Caribbean area also included the islands of Guadeloupe and Martinique, became French departments and sent deputies to the French Assembly. In 1894 a minister for the colonies was appointed to carry out French colonial policy. This was essentially to model the culture, education, and economy of the colonies along French lines and to turn all inhabitants into French citizens. It was a policy known as "assimilation."

The citizens, however, had little experience of politics, and many still could not read or write. Fraud and intimidation were commonplace, and in the legislative elections of 1924 and 1928 this became very obvious. In 1906 a businessman, Jean Galmont, had arrived in the colony. He was a good employer, paying his men a just price for their work. Elsewhere the conditions for workers were very bad, and in some work yards there was a death rate of up to one-fourth of the labor force. Galmont determined to do something about this and he was elected a deputy in 1919. In the fraudulent elections of 1924 someone unknown was elected in his place, and the same thing happened in 1929. For three days after these elections, the Guianese erupted into violence. Then Galmont was murdered and more violence followed with lootings and fires. Six of Galmont's political opponents also were murdered.

Life returned to normality, and in 1931 the lawyer G. Monnerville, the same person who later helped bring about the abolition of the penal colony, was elected deputy. World War II broke out in 1939, and for much of the time during the war the colony was cut off from France. These new circumstances forced French Guiana to fend for itself, and more effort was put into the agricultural economy. The war brought about a change in attitudes both in France and in its colonies. Several African colonies demanded and got independence. French Guiana, now suitably "French" in every way, became an overseas department of France in 1946, with the same laws, regulations, and administration as a department in the home country.

OVERSEAS DEPARTMENT OF FRANCE

Although it had acquired a new status, French Guiana continued to be a political and economic backwater until the 1970s. Then a pro-independence group emerged, and racial tension developed between the Guianese and some immigrant workers. These tensions, combined with a deteriorating economic situation, resulted in violent demonstrations against French rule. France's answer was to grant regional status to French Guiana in 1974, at the same time introducing strict security measures and more economic aid, particularly by way of investment. In the same year there were demonstrations against unemployment, and several trade unionists and pro-independence politicians were arrested.

The economic situation did not improve, partly owing to the problems of developing the forested interior of the country. In the late 1970s about one-third of the population was unemployed. The leading political party, the *Parti Socialist Guyanais* (PSG) called for more autonomy for the country to run its own affairs, a campaign supported by most of the population. But a minority of separatists demanded nothing short of full independence. In 1980 there were a number of bomb attacks against "colonial" and government targets by an extremist group called *Fo nou Libèrè la Guyana* (FNLG). Three years later more small-scale bomb attacks were thought to be the responsibility of a terrorist group from Guadeloupe, anxious to spread its campaign for independence throughout France's Caribbean territories.

In 1982 and 1983 reforms introduced by the French Socialist government led to the formation of a new regional council with increased responsibility for economic, social, and cultural affairs. French Guiana responded in 1988 by giving Francois Mitterand 60 percent of its vote in the French presidential election. Throughout the 1980s and into the 1990s, the PSG has been the dominant political party in French Guiana with a majority in both the regional and general councils. In regional council elections in 1992 the PSG won sixteen seats, while the major party, the *Front Democratique Guyanais*, won ten.

Apart from the separatist independence issue, the other major problem recently has been illegal immigration. In 1986-1988 up to ten thousand Surinamese refugees fled from civil war in their own country into French Guiana. In 1989 French troops were brought in to patrol the border. The Surinamese believed that French

Guiana was planning an invasion, and the relationship between the two countries deteriorated. In the same year there was a dramatic increase in violent crime that the Guianese blamed on immigrants and refugees, particularly the Surinamese. In protest there have been many strikes and demonstrations, with demands for more police and stricter immigration controls.

Kourou and the space center present another problem. Economically it is French Guiana's main center of investment and activity. It provides considerable employment for local people in construction and some town services. In effect, though, Kourou is a mainly white, middle-class French town of some fourteen thousand people in the middle of a mostly undeveloped, mixed Creole-black-Indian state. There are plans, too, to double the population of the town by the end of the twentieth century. The authorities, recognizing the problem, launched the Phèdre plan in 1989. This plan aims to ensure that the town's wealth is spread throughout the country. So far it has met with little success. Kourou remains exempt from taxes, and many see it as a modern symbol of Guiana's legendary corruption.

GOVERNMENT

French Guiana is governed according to the provisions of the French constitution as an overseas department of France, with additional status as a region of France. It sends two elected deputies to the French National Assembly in Paris, and one elected representative to the French Senate. French Guiana is also represented at the European Parliament in Strasbourg.

The head of state is the president of France. In French Guiana the administration is headed by a prefect (governor) appointed by

Fanlike traveler's palm trees stand in front of the Prefecture in Cayenne.

France. To deal with local affairs, there are two legislative bodies: a general council of nineteen members and a regional council of thirty-one members. All adults have the right to vote. French Guiana is divided into two *arrondissements,* "political subdivisions," Cayenne and Saint-Laurent du Maroni, each administered by a subprefect. The arrondissements are divided into *communes,* of which there are twenty-one, each with its own elected municipal council headed by a mayor.

The administration of justice is carried out through local courts of appeal, the *Tribuneaux d'Instance,* and at a higher level, the *Tribuneaux de Grande Instance.* The highest court of appeal however, is the *Cour d'Appel,* based in Fort-de-France, the capital of the French Caribbean island of Martinique.

DEPARTMENTAL DEFENSE

France maintains a military force of about three thousand in French Guiana including a regiment of French Legionnaires, whose principal task is to protect the space installation in Kourou. There is a departmental police force. In response to the protests of 1989, the size of the police force was doubled with the arrival of one hundred French riot police.

Chapter 5

THE PEOPLES
OF FRENCH GUIANA

THE FIRST PEOPLE

North and South America were settled first by people who migrated from Central Asia sometime during the Ice Age. During this period, with the lowering of the world's oceans, a land bridge was exposed where the Bering Strait now separates Alaska and Siberia. Early humans lived in the plains and uplands of Mexico and the Andes. There they hunted the last of the large animals, such as the wild horses and ground sloths. As the large mammals became extinct, the hunters had to rely on smaller prey such as deer and the ancestors of the llamas and alpacas. They also collected wild berries, seeds, and roots.

Migration into the lowlands began about 8000 B.C. Small groups moved to the coasts and along the rivers where there were plenty of fish and some edible wild plants. Life was essentially nomadic, but where food was plentiful large numbers gathered. In time, over several thousand years, some cultivation of root crops took place. "Shifting cultivation," whereby plots are abandoned after a few years to allow them to regain their fertility, combined with hunting, gathering, and fishing, has remained the basis of existence for the lowland forest people. *Petroglyphs*, or simple pictures carved on rock, are among the few relics they left.

The arrival of the Europeans in the sixteenth century severely disrupted this harmonious way of life, and it was at this time that the people became known as "Indians." They acquired this misnomer because Columbus thought he had reached India.

By the eighteenth century the Indian population was estimated at around twenty-five thousand, although their number was, and still is, very difficult to determine. The arrival of the Europeans led to hostilities between the two sides. But the Indians' most powerful enemies were new diseases unwittingly introduced by the foreigners. Normally healthy Indians had no resistance to smallpox, measles, cholera, tuberculosis, or influenza.

The most important group of Indians was the Galibi, with a reputation as fierce warriors and cannibals. They, together with the Arawaks, were the first to encounter the Europeans. The number of Galibi dropped from about five or six thousand at the beginning of the seventeenth century to around four hundred by the mid-nineteenth century. In the interior, commercial trading along the Oyapock River also brought the Indians into contact with Europeans. Devastating epidemics spread through some of the Jesuit missions, leaving thousands dead. The Oyampi and Emerillon tribes who entered French Guiana between 1815 and 1817 were fleeing from the Portuguese in Brazil and were similarly reduced.

THE INDIANS

Six tribes of Indians have survived in French Guiana: in the coastal region are the Galibi, the Arawak, and the Palikur, and in

A Galibi village near Mana

the interior are the Wayana, the Emerillon, and the Oyampi.

The Galibi is the largest group in the coastal region. Most live near Saint-Laurent du Maroni and Mana. Smaller numbers of Arawak are concentrated near Cayenne and near Saint-Laurent du Maroni. Both peoples are to an extent Westernized, with Western-style clothing including shorts and T-shirts, and many have been converted to the Catholic Church. The Galibi in particular have increased their number by marriage with Creoles, who make up the bulk of the population. In some villages, a few Galibis still live traditionally by fishing, some hunting, and agriculture, but most prefer to be part of French Guiana's cash economy where possible, doing a job from which they can earn money.

The Palikur live in isolated family groups near the town of Roura and in the region of the Oyapock River. They too have adopted Western dress, but have little other interest in life outside their own villages. Few speak Creole or French, and they seem to have no desire to integrate further into French Guianese life.

One visitor to the hundred or so Emerillon Indians living close to the Maroni River has described them as almost completely destroyed. Their villages were dirty and disorganized, and the few remaining members of the tribe have turned to alcohol and prostitution. A similar situation is found in Camopi, a settlement of thatch and corrugated iron huts at the confluence of the Camopi and Oyapock Rivers. There Emerillon and Oyampi Indians live separately in two villages opposite some bars set up by Brazilians on their side of the river.

By contrast two hundred or so Oyampis who live in the upper reaches of the Oyapock, some twelve hours upriver from Camopi, are the most untouched of French Guiana's Indians. They produce most of what they need and do not have much contact with Creoles, only occasionally selling fish to traders when they have a need for cash. It is woman's work to tend the gardens and grow manioc, yams, sweet potatoes, sugarcane, cotton, and bananas, while the men fish, hunt, and clear the forest for planting. Dress is a modest wraparound skirt patterned or dyed bright red, and occasionally they paint their bodies. Much of their traditional culture, however, such as pottery making, the use of feathers, and knowledge of their myths and legends, has largely disappeared or been forgotten.

The Wayanas of the upper reaches of the Maroni River originally came from Brazil and are now the largest of the interior tribes, though there are fewer than one thousand of them. The Wayana also are known as the Roucouennes, after *roucou,* the French word for the annatto red dye used to paint their bodies.

The Wayanas live in several villages scattered along the river, typically in a small open area cleared by slash-and-burn methods during the October dry season. Each village has a *tukusipan,* a

Left: The Wayana attach a painted maluana *to the ceiling of the communal hut.*
Right: Young boys, wearing kalimbes, *meet their French schoolteacher.*

large communal hut used by the Indians for special gatherings and ceremonies. The tukusipan is circular and palm thatched. Attached to the ceiling, which is no more than the underside of the thatch, there is the *maluana*, a large wooden disk cut from a cross section of the trunk of a fromager tree. The disk is painted with depictions of forest animals such as anteaters, frogs, centipedes, or birds, which for the Indians represent spirits, the mythical beings of good and evil.

Men wear a *kalimbe*, a red loincloth drawn between the legs and fastened around the waist. The women go naked above the waist and wear either a *kamisa*, a wraparound skirt similar to the Oyampi's, or a *weyu*, a form of cotton apron that leaves their bottoms exposed. Recently some have taken to wearing Western-style underpants beneath the weyu.

Manioc, the cassava plant, is the most important basic crop. It can be turned into food and a drink. In its natural state, manioc is

A Wayana woman collects ripe manioc, which is made into a large, thin bread called cassava.

poisonous, but the Wayana have known for generations how to make it safe and edible. The process is started when the women and young children scrape the manioc tubers to remove the brown skin. Then the pieces of tuber, now glistening white and moist, are grated. The grated manioc, coarse and damp with the poison, is stuffed into a long flexible basket the Wayana call a *tinkii*, a remarkable device used by many Amazon Indians. When the tinkii is full of grated manioc it is stretched so that when it contracts, the poisonous juice is squeezed out. Lumps of compressed but almost dry manioc are removed from the tinkii and sifted by hand to make a "flour" that is spread on a large, circular earthenware plate heated over a log fire. The flour is formed into a large, biscuit-thin cake or bread called *cassava* that after drying in the sun is eaten with soups and meat. The Wayanas also make their favorite drink, *cashiri*, by boiling manioc and allowing it to ferment.

A Wayana man relaxes with his daughter.

The Indians get their protein from the forest, where they catch or shoot many of the wild animals, or from the rivers, where they catch fish. At one time the Wayana used bows and arrows for fishing or they drugged the fish with the juice of a jungle vine. But today they use a modern rod and line. Sometimes they set nets with floats in the rivers near the riverbanks.

One traditional custom retained by the Wayana is *marake,* the "ant test." It takes place when a boy or girl reaches the age of eleven or twelve, to mark the beginning of adulthood. A wicker frame with as many stinging ants inserted in it as possible is applied all over the child's body. Although it is a painful experience, the child is expected to remain silent.

Most of the Wayana live inside the *zone interdite,* the "prohibited" zone, which covers much of the southern part of the country. Here travel is forbidden to anyone without a permit, and visitors need a medical certificate to ensure they are not carrying

Wayana with their handmade canoes at the edge of the Maroni River.
Inset: Jean-Paul, a teacher from France, gives a math lesson.

infectious diseases, particularly lung infections. The French government has a positive approach to the side-by-side coexistence of Indian life and modern society. The villages are not totally isolated from the material goods and development of the modern world, so a typical Wayana wears a digital watch or owns a cassette player. The Wayana wife uses aluminum pots and has sharp stainless steel knives from France. The hunter has a French or perhaps Brazilian shotgun and shells. The children have toys from the supermarket in Cayenne, and the teenage girls use makeup. Many Indian families now have canoes with powerful outboard motors, often paid for by working as guides to French geologists and engineers exploring the interior for minerals.

Schools have been established with teachers who travel on contract from France. At the village of Twenke, Jean-Paul Klingelhofer, from Alsace, and his wife Françoise have lived with the Wayana for twenty years. Jean-Paul and Françoise took four years to learn the Wayana language, which they now use every day. Jean-Paul teaches French and other subjects in the school and Françoise runs the dispensary, where she treats many common ailments.

Twenke is a center of activity for several Wayana communities, and the French government provides money for the infrastructure. Children from other villages travel by canoe each day to Jean-Paul's school, which even has a television set for showing videos. The power comes from batteries charged by solar panels that also provide light for the dispensary and some of the houses. For more than twenty years Twenke has had purified running water. The Wayana can draw the water from several taps located around the village.

Another Frenchman who has lived among the Wayana even longer than Jean-Paul is becoming something of a legend. Andre Cognat, a one-time steelworker from Lyons, France, set out in 1961 at the age of twenty-three to explore South America. After his boat capsized in the Maroni River, he was rescued by two Wayana Indians, who "adopted" him. He married into the tribe and founded a settlement called Antecuma. Over the years he has introduced medicine, dentistry, and education. Cognat also has become well known as a spokesman for the rights of the Wayana people.

THE MAROONS

Late in the eighteenth century when slaves were running away from the Dutch plantations and taking refuge in the forest, some of the marrons, or fugitives, crossed the Maroni River and settled on the French bank. The largest group are the Bonis, and they are

Bosch children outside their home (left) and Bonis shopping in the market (right)

all French citizens. Other groups include the Bosch (or Djukas), the Paramacas, and the Saramacas, many of whom have arrived recently as a result of the troubles in Suriname. The Bonis and the Bosch do not get along, for a reason that dates from colonial days.

Some of the earliest slaves to escape remained free and independent for so long that the Dutch authorities were forced to make their peace with them. In exchange for their freedom, these slaves, which included some of the Bosch, agreed to hunt down and return other escaping slaves to the authorities. In 1788 they caught and beheaded Aluku Nenge dit Boni, a well-regarded rebel leader. His followers, who named themselves Bonis after him, have never forgiven this act.

The principal riverside villages of the Maroons are Grand Santi, Papaichton (also called Pompidouville after French President Georges Pompidou), and Apatou. Houses are made of wood and palm thatch, with doors painted with highly colorful, psychedelic patterns. The communities are largely self-sufficient, and while the women look after the home and domestic needs, the men work on the river as guides and canoeists. They have a reputation as excellent boatmen and have unparalleled experience of the rapids in the Maroni.

The Maroons have their own language, Taki-Taki, which is a mixture of their original African dialect and English and Dutch words. They also have retained some of their African cultural traditions, such as "The Great Man," who is their civil and spiritual leader. Like the Indians, though, a question begins to arise over their future. While the Bonis and Bosch who remain on the river seem likely to retain their individuality and culture, there is rising concern because many of the young now prefer to head for Cayenne and other centers, in search of a different way of life.

THE IMMIGRANTS

In the past two hundred years immigrants arrived in French Guiana from many parts of the world. Among the first were Lebanese and Chinese, followed by East Indians, people from Reunion Island in the Indian Ocean, Moroccans, Laotians, Haitians, Brazilians, Vietnamese, and West Indians from the French Caribbean islands, some of whom arrived at the beginning of the twentieth century after the huge eruption of Mount Pelée in Martinique. The most recent immigrants are refugees from Suriname. There also are the French, known as *Les Metros,* who come from the home country, metropolitan France.

The Haitians fled to French Guiana to escape the bad conditions in their homeland, the poorest country in the New World, and most live in Cayenne working as hired labor. The Brazilians are

Hmong women in their traditional Laotian clothes (left)
and the Hmong settlement in Cacao (right)

associated mainly with the construction industry, where they can earn more money than in Brazil. Most of the Asians are involved in commerce, and there are many Chinese restaurants in Cayenne and other towns. The Chinese also own the majority of the numerous self-service stores known as *libre service*, which close only on Sunday afternoons. Now in their fourth or fifth generation, the Lebanese are particularly well integrated, running textile and clothing industries and playing an active part in politics.

In 1977 a group of five hundred Hmongs, political refugees from Laos, arrived and settled in the village of Cacao, which previously was a small prison settlement. Cacao on the Comte River lies at the foot of a range of forested hills almost 1,000 feet (305 meters) high and some 30 miles (48 kilometers) south of Cayenne. Although there was opposition from many Creoles, Hmongs received local and government help to clear the forest, cultivate rice, and start market gardening, growing a variety of

Above: A camp in Saint-Laurent used for Surinamese refugees.
Right: Ronnie Brunswijk, leader of the Surinamese rebels

fruits and vegetables. A second group of Hmongs arrived ten years later and settled near Saint-Laurent du Maroni. Today these industrious people are able to supply almost half of the local market, and *maracudja,* or passion fruit, is grown exclusively by them.

Sadly, their success is marred by the fact that many of the younger Hmongs do not wish to be farmers and are leaving the village for Cayenne or the United States. The community has retained its identity, however. Restaurants in Cacao offer excellent Asian meals.

In the 1980s it was estimated that one-fourth of French Guiana's population was made up of illegal immigrants. Concern grew with the strain imposed on health and education services together with an increase in crime. In 1986 civil war broke out in Suriname between the military-backed government and rebels led by Ronnie Brunswijk. Several thousand of Brunswijk's supporters, mainly Saramaca Maroons, fled to French Guiana. At one time thought to number ten thousand, and now probably around seven thousand, the refugees live in poor conditions in camps around Saint-Laurent du Maroni. After a peace agreement between the Suriname rebels and the government in 1991, the refugees were offered a unique opportunity. They could return to their own country, under French surveillance, to vote. Many preferred not to go and stayed on. In 1992, the French government implemented a program by which all refugees from Suriname were offered financial incentives to return to Suriname.

THE CREOLES

By far the largest group of people, over two-thirds of the population, are Creoles, which by their own definition means half-castes who have their origins among the Africans, whites, and many immigrant peoples who have settled in the country. Within Creole society there are poor and wealthy, although the majority are middle-class people. Their dress suits the climate, mainly T-shirts and jeans, and even businesspeople are quite informal. Occasionally, Paris fashions are seen. Although French is the official language, the Creoles frequently use their own dialect, made up of assorted African and French mixed with some English and Brazilian words.

The Creole community has developed since the abolition of slavery and the introduction of the French assimilation policy. From owning small plots of land and leading a self-sufficient existence, Creoles now are employed in every level of French Guianese society as teachers, civil servants, taxi drivers, politicians, and in the legal and medical professions. The majority live and work in Cayenne, which offers facilities and amenities, particularly for education and health, that cannot easily be found elsewhere.

Chapter 6

LIVING IN
FRENCH GUIANA

FRENCH GUIANESE AT WORK

Many people in French Guiana enjoy a high standard of living. In the late 1980s the country is said to have led France in the consumption of champagne. Shiny Citroen, Peugeot, and Renault cars swish up and down the major highway. The majority of people have good homes and television sets. Yet in most respects French Guiana is far less developed than almost all of its neighbors.

This curious situation arises because French Guiana is very heavily subsidized by the French government. The state is the country's largest employer, providing more than two-thirds of all jobs, with many people working in some form of administration. The space center at Kourou is the country's second-largest employer, although most of the work on site is carried out by foreign technicians and scientists. The program does, however, provide secondary work in which the French Guianese are

Avenue Charles de Gaulle in Cayenne (above), a restaurant specializing in Chinese food (below), and a cayenne pepper (right), the hot red pepper after which Cayenne is named

involved, particularly in construction. Expansion in the early 1990s created more jobs, and hundreds of people, many of them from neighboring countries, found employment. Unemployment among the French Guianese remains high, however, largely because they prefer work that does not involve manual labor.

CAYENNE

The name *Cayenne* comes from the hot red pepper that is grown here. The peppers have been exported from French Guiana as far back as the seventeenth century.

A first impression of Cayenne is of a French town with *gendarmes*, "police officers," in blue uniforms, baguettes and croissants in the bakeries, fine window displays of French fashions, and copies of leading French newspapers—although a few days old. The main street is called Avenue Charles de Gaulle. But it is not the "Paris of the Atlantic," as one leading French academic called it, not least because of the oppressive heat, the tropical rain forest that surrounds the town, the predominantly Creole population speaking their own dialect, the numerous Chinese restaurants, and the many signs with Asian names.

More than 35 percent of French Guiana's population lives in Cayenne, with a further 20 percent in its suburbs of Remire, Montjoly, and Matoury. At the center of the old city is the Place Léopold Heder, also known as Place de Grenoble, which still retains something of its colonial atmosphere. To one side of the square is a Jesuit-built residence, now restored with fine colonnades. Called *l'Hôtel de la Préfecture*, it is the residence of the prefect of Guyane. An attractive fountain in front of the Prefecture is surrounded by fanlike traveler's palms, mango trees, and

Cayenne ★

Some scenes of Cayenne are the main square, Place des Palmistes (above); young people on their motorcycles (below left); and the post and telephone office (below right).

Statue of Felix Eboué

hibiscus. La Poste, the French office that acts as a bank and a post office, is opposite.

Nearby is another square, the Place des Palmistes, shaded by neatly arranged rows of royal palms, some more than sixty-five feet (twenty meters) high and dominated by the statue of Felix Eboué, perhaps French Guiana's most famous son. He organized support in French Equatorial Africa, where he was governor, for General de Gaulle's Free French forces in World War II. On the square there are air-conditioned stores, businesses, a theater, and one of Cayenne's favorite meeting places, the Cafe des Palmistes, complete with wrought-iron balconies brought from France in colonial times, tropical slatted windows, and corrugated iron roof.

The old central part of Cayenne is a jumble of three- and four-story timber buildings, multicolored shops and houses, with

Buildings in the old section of Cayenne (left); boats along the Canal Laussant (above)

shutters missing, slats swinging in the wind, and rusting ironwork lining the avenues and streets. The rigid plan of avenues that cross the town from east to west and streets that run from north to south make it easy to get around central Cayenne. The Canal Laussant, a dike built in 1777 by Governor Malouet, cuts across the town from east to west only four blocks from the Place de Palmistes. The fish market is beside the canal, and around it is a colorful area known as the *crique*, meaning "creek." A few boats are kept in the crique and there is plenty of activity. On the other side of the canal is the Chinese quarter, with its commercial stores and businesses of all kinds, including places for smoking fish and meat, and numerous small restaurants, mostly Chinese and Indonesian, that serve snacks and meals.

The entrance to the Guianese Space Center in Kourou

KOUROU

In 1964 the French government chose the site of Kourou for its space program in preference to thirteen other sites around the world. Heavier loads can be sent into orbit around the earth from an equatorial zone, and Kourou's excellent location makes it the only launch base in the world to have a launch angle of 104 degrees over the sea (from 10.5 degrees west to 93.5 degrees east of due north). This means that the launches into both east-west and north-south orbits can be made without endangering any nearby population.

The old town of Kourou, known as Kourou *bourg*, is close to the river Kourou and began as a settlement tied to the logging trade. The streets are narrow and lined with small restaurants and Chinese-run stores. Not far from the river there is a village where

Shopping district in Kourou (above); tourists arriving on the hydrofoil after a visit to Devil's Island (below)

The old section of Kourou

a few Maroon families live. The old harbor is nearby and still holds a few small fishing boats, but the area is mostly devoted to the yachts and other craft owned by the wealthier Kourouciens or the engineers and technicians of the space center. A daily hydrofoil also takes visitors to the Iles du Salut.

The new Kourou was built alongside the old, with new roads and a new harbor, Pariacabo, on the river with a small trading sector nearby. The buildings are essentially French in design and use modern materials, including painted pressed-metal roofing and plate glass. Rows of two- or three-story apartments are set in gardens around a lake where there are parking spaces for cars, carefully sited stores, boutiques, a supermarket, and bars. New administrative buildings, banks with automatic cash machines, a disco, and a cinema give the appearance of a planned European town. There is even a rush hour as hundreds of engineers head to and from work by car.

Facilities for the space center are spread around the entire area, and the *Center Spatial Guyanese* (CSG) owns much of the land along the coast in the direction of Sinnamary, as well as the Iles du Salut where a rocket-tracking station has been established.

The Jupiter control room of the Space Center

About 2.5 miles (4 kilometers) from Kourou on the old road to Sinnamary stands the technical center with administrative offices, the space museum, and the "Jupiter Control Room," with its rows of computer and television monitors. The launch sites and tall rocket assembly buildings are 6 miles (10 kilometers) farther along the same road, which is open to public traffic at all times except for the crucial few hours before and during a launch.

One little piece of history remains on a small headland near Kourou. It is a small white tower, known as the Dreyfus Tower. During World War I, semaphore signals were sent from the tower to get news of prisoner Captain Dreyfus and to make sure he was still there and had not been rescued by German gunboats.

The border town of Saint-Georges de l'Oyapock

OTHER COMMUNITIES

Outside the two centers of Cayenne and Kourou there is relatively little opportunity for employment. Along the coast to the east of Cayenne, there used to be work, first with the sugar industry in the nineteenth century. Later there were the gold discoveries in the Approuague River region, which gave life to the ports of the coast. But agricultural production slowed up as heavy rains made it difficult to use big machines on the lowland marshes, and today there is little gold. Some hamlets have survived on the Oyapock River, mainly by fishing. Saint-Georges de l'Oyapock stays in business as the border town with Brazil. But it is small, with less than two thousand people, and totally isolated from the rest of the country except for regular air service by Air Guyane and barges that transport goods from Cayenne by sea and river.

A church in Mana

In the coastal lowlands west of Cayenne and Kourou are several small towns. Sinnamary was quite prosperous at the time of the gold rush. Today it hopes for investment in agriculture and more spin-off from the space center. Farther west is Iracoubo with nearby Galibi Indian villages and the larger towns of Mana and Saint-Laurent du Maroni. Once the administrative center of the penal colony, Saint-Laurent today is a quiet colonial town of about fourteen thousand people. Many relics of the period remain, when there was ample labor to build houses and roads. Parts of the prison camps are being renovated as historic monuments, and the mostly dilapidated prison hospital has some improved sections for present-day use.

The busiest part of Saint-Laurent is near the river where the Bonis have their pirogues. A small quay is the center of traffic trading up and down the Maroni River. From the same place

A municipal building in Saint-Laurent

there is a ferry connection with Albina across the river in Suriname. Men, mainly from the Maroon communities, are busy packing very large pirogues, some over fifty feet (over fifteen meters) long and powered by outboard motors. All kinds of goods, including most commonly drums of oil, bags of rice, alcohol, and cigarettes, are carried by river into the interior, and fruit, coconuts, and even some gold are brought out. Little else happens in Saint-Laurent. Despite talk of turning it into a tourist center, so far plans discussed by the authorities have come to little.

Outside the towns most people get only occasional salaried work, so they have to be self-sufficient. In gardens alongside their simple houses they grow coconuts; fruit such as mangoes, lemons, and oranges; and vegetables and spices. Some keep chickens. Small farmers also grow manioc and other crops such as sweet

Schoolchildren of Saint-Georges de l'Oyapock

potatoes, corn, and bananas. Small farms are generally located in small clearings in the forest, and crops usually are moved from one area to another over the years.

EDUCATION

Education in French Guiana is modeled on the French system, and by law all children should attend school. Pupils attend primary level for five years beginning at the age of six, and secondary level from the age of eleven to sixteen. At the end of secondary school, students take examinations, but compared with France, where at least half the pupils reach that level, only 23 percent reach the same grade in French Guiana.

In 1990 more than thirty thousand students attended school. This is a significant increase over previous years and is due partly to the influx of immigrants in the country and partly to a growth in the birth rate. Between 1974 and 1986 the number of children

The University Antilles-Guyane

attending primary school increased from around seven thousand
to almost seventeen thousand. The total enrollment in secondary
schools during that period doubled. This put a severe strain on
the educational system, and many new schools have been built.
Most ambitious is the recently completed Lycée Vidal in Cayenne,
a massive, modern construction that offers students all possible
facilities. Education is free, but a small percentage of students do
attend private school for which tuition is charged.

School lessons are much the same as in Europe or the United
States, with mathematics, science, economics, history, and
geography among the most important subjects. Students who wish
to go on to higher education can attend a university in France or
a branch of the University Antilles-Guyane in Cayenne, where the
most popular courses are in law, economics, and administration.
Other colleges offer higher courses in technical studies,
agriculture, and teacher-training. The adult illiteracy rate is 18
percent, which is high by today's standards in Latin America.

The interior of the church of St. Joseph in Iracoubo was painted by a former convict.

RELIGION

The Jesuits, with other missionaries and priests, introduced Catholicism into French Guiana in the seventeenth century, and it has remained the predominant religion ever since. About three-quarters of the population belong to the Roman Catholic Church. The highest appointed cleric is the bishop of Cayenne, whose diocese of Cayenne is part of the archdiocese of Fort-de-France in Martinique.

The French Guianese are free to practice the religion of their choice, and other Christian churches include the Anglican, Seventh-Day Adventist, Assembly of God, the Church of Jesus Christ of Latter-Day Saints (Mormon), and Jehovah's Witnesses. Immigrant communities have retained their own faiths. Buddhism and Islam are practiced among the East Indians and southeast Asians, while the Maroons and Indians follow their individual spiritual beliefs that have been passed down through the generations.

Tropical diseases are studied at the Institut Pasteur.

HEALTH AND SOCIAL WELFARE

The Institut Pasteur, located in Cayenne, is renowned throughout Latin America. It undertakes research into tropical diseases. Some, like yellow fever, have been eradicated from French Guiana, while the incidence of malaria and leprosy have been reduced.

In 1991-92 there were 200 physicians, 32 dentists, and 31 midwives working in French Guiana, some in the principal hospitals in Cayenne and Kourou and others in the dispensaries that exist in every commune. The improvement in medical care, together with good diets, has led to a considerable growth in the birth rate, which in 1992 was 29 per thousand as against a death rate of 4 per thousand. This increase is welcomed because one of French Guiana's major problems for so long has been its tiny population, but it poses problems in maintaining educational and health standards for everybody.

French Guiana has a system of social security similar to that in France. It provides payments for work injury, unemployment, and maternity, as well as family and disability allowances. There are four trade unions. The largest, the *Union des Travailleurs Guyanais*, "the Workers' Union" (UTG), represents many immigrant workers. It has organized a number of strikes to protest against low pay and the poor conditions of immigrants working on some of the country's development projects, including the expansion of the space base in Kourou. A strike in 1991 was unsuccessful when the union tried to delay the launch of a rocket by preventing technicians from getting to the base.

FOOD

Food in French Guiana, whether at the international level, with French cuisine, or Chinese and other Asian cuisines, or in the home, is good and plentiful. Stores are stocked with imported French foods such as cheeses from Normandy, other dairy products, pâté from Alsace, and meat, tomatoes, and vegetables, all of which are flown in once or twice a week from France. Beverages including Coca-Cola canned in Belgium, beer from several European countries, and of course many kinds of French wine, arrive regularly by sea.

Rice, yams, breadfruit, and *couac*, a flour made from manioc, are the basic foodstuffs in Creole cooking, spiced with green lemons, peppers, nutmeg, and Cayenne pepper. There are vegetables and many kinds of fruit, but it is the huge variety of fish together with game from the forest that enables the Guianese to produce truly individual dishes, such as boiled caiman or anaconda

A shopper buys some lettuce at the central market in Cayenne.

fricassée with red beans. Slightly more conventional, but very typical, is shark or *blaff de poisson*, fish poached in wine and lemon juice, with onions, spices, and a whole chili.

HOUSING

Most houses in French Guiana are constructed of wood and have corrugated iron roofs, which offer protection against both the sun and extremely heavy rains. But times are changing, and more investment from the government and regional development councils has led to an increasing variety of modern three- or four-story apartments, rows of well-designed bungalows, and small houses of many kinds. Even the distant towns have a few new houses, some of which are sold partly built so that they are cheaper and can be completed by purchasers in their own time. Many are brightly painted and contrast with the otherwise rural

Above: Housing in Maripasoula, a three- or four-day
upriver journey on the Maroni River from Saint-Laurent
Below: Low-cost housing in Cayenne

Wayana schoolchildren from the village of Twenke on their way to school

aspect. By contrast, some coastal Indians live in thatch and wood "carbets," which have a roof but no walls, to allow for ventilation. The same style is used by small farmers as temporary shelters in the forest when they need to spend time on their plots of land.

The Wayana houses are of simple palm thatch built on short posts above the ground to keep them dry in case of flooding and to protect them from forest rodents and crawling insects. Hammocks are the main pieces of "furniture," and like all Indian homes, every corner of the roof is stuffed with something useful such as bows and arrows, old baskets, and cloth.

Recently the government has begun to subsidize some new housing for the Wayanas. A few now have new wooden houses under a scheme in which the government pays for sawn timber and other materials and the community does the work. In Saint-Laurent du Maroni many of the Bonis live in a village of wooden houses with a distinctly African style, complete with doors painted with Boni designs. This suburb, known as *La Charbonnière*, is close to the river and is another area of regional development.

Some participants in the Cayenne Carnival

Chapter 7

CARNIVAL AND CRAFTS

Culture and folklore in French Guiana have their origins mainly in African and West Indian traditions, but the influence of France and many of the immigrant communities also is evident. For example, the strictly European dances such as the waltz, the mazurka, and the quadrille remain popular. However, there is no national symphony orchestra and no ballet. Local artists rarely exhibit and local writers are not well known, even in France. The only literary figure of distinction was León Damas, a poet, who led the Caribbean *modernismo* movement of the 1920s.

The best-known music is reggae and other styles from the Caribbean with African influence. Brazilian music is often heard on the radio, and Brazilian parties, or *festas,* are becoming more and more popular. The Hmongs celebrate their new year in October, and the Wayana have celebrations at the end of the year. But the largest festival in the country is Carnival, which takes place in Cayenne. Carnival traditionally marks the beginning of Lent, but it starts some weeks earlier.

CARNIVAL

Carnival time is when the Creole love of music and dancing really comes alive, above all to the beat of African and Caribbean

Masked touloulous *woman*

rhythms. A particular favorite is the *casse-co,* a dance accompanied only by drums that the dancer can interpret as freely as he or she pleases. Celebrations preceding Carnival start from the first Sunday after Epiphany (January 6), and all take their cue from the masked and disguised women, the *touloulous,* who appear in the streets. Each weekend the dance halls are filled with people dancing the *touffé yen yen,* a sort of close combat that goes on until dawn, when the musicians pile onto a truck and make for the marketplace for a breakfast of blaff de poisson and *peté pie,* a drink made of rum, sugarcane, and the herbal leaf of wormwood, which is also used in absinthe and vermouth.

Each Sunday before Ash Wednesday, the beginning of Lent, the touloulous proceed through the streets of Cayenne shouting and gesticulating to the sound of assorted musical instruments, sometimes including steel bands. Watching over them is a guard of Maroons, whose bodies are completely covered in black soot

94

During Carnival the Maroons (left) cover themselves with black soot and oil and the touloulous *(right) use many different kinds of masks.*

and oil. An advance guard throws flour into the crowds over the children, who scream and shout with delight and fear. Among the dancers are those with the masks of death, the *lan-mo*. Then there are the *balayeuses*, women with silk scarves covering their heads. They mime the work of their ancestors who used to sweep the streets. The *bobis* represent a sort of dull, heavy bear, and the sugarcane cutters represent the world of work. The crowd follows behind, dancing frenetically to the music of a band playing from the back of a truck.

Some Carnival days have a particular theme. Shrove Tuesday, the day before Ash Wednesday, is the day of the she-devils, when all the dancers are spectacularly dressed in red. On Ash Wednesday everyone wears black and white costumes, and the *Vaval*, the soul and king of Carnival in the form of a rag doll, is burned and buried in the Place des Palmistes.

95

CRAFTS

It is perhaps surprising that despite the numerous different cultures, French Guiana is not rich with handicrafts. The woods from the forests are the most popular materials, and wood turning with modern tools produces some fine work. The favorites are decorative bowls, containers of many kinds, and cups. Often the craftspeople mix woods of different colors: purple, yellow, mahogany, or veined with green, and then work the piece until it is beautifully polished. Also using wood, the Maroons make finely carved animals, plates with curious designs, and the locally famous Aloukou chairs, literally "Maroon chairs."

The Hmongs have a small trade with crafts such as their red-and-black embroidered cloth. Other designs are based on their daily life. Cacao is one of the centers for a trade in the brilliant butterflies of the forest, especially the morphos. The butterflies are caught and killed, and then their iridescent wings with many hues are placed together carefully to create pictures. Usually the picture is held firmly behind glass in a frame.

But perhaps the most ambitious handicraft program has been that introduced by Jean-Paul Klingelhofer to the Wayana. *Culture Artisat Wayana* (CAWAY) is a handicraft-producing cooperative. As well as the necklaces and bracelets they make from "pearls," or glass trade beads, the Indians have traditionally made fine products from forest materials. For CAWAY they produce baskets and sieves from split cane, bows, arrows, necklaces of seeds, examples of the maluana from their meeting house, and pottery made from a yellow clay that they color before baking in the sun. When aluminum goods first arrived on the upper Maroni, the Indians stopped making pots, but CAWAY is reviving the craft.

Above: A Wayana woman is shaping a handmade earthenware pot made from yellow clay. Below: Hmong Laotian women make detailed picture-story embroidery.

A Wayana man braids palm leaves to make a mat or rug.

The women spin and weave cotton, both for clothing and for hammocks, while the men do basketwork.

The Wayana's handmade goods are traded by CAWAY mostly in Cayenne through a small shop in the town. Tourist visits to the villages are discouraged, but trade in the shop is usually brisk, especially among visitors from France. The Wayana are glad to earn money that gives them a chance to buy many goods, especially the prized outboard motors for their canoes. Yet despite these changes they still live quite simply from the forest and are proud of their traditions.

RECREATION

The larger towns have organized sports grounds, and soccer is popular everywhere, even in some Indian communities. As in France, cycling has an enthusiastic following, both as relaxation and as a competitive sport for which weekend road races are

Cyclists in a road race

organized. The less energetic who look for simpler pleasures in their spare time often play *boules*, a French game of skill using heavy metal balls.

Although there is no local tradition of using the beaches and sea for leisure, the Metros in Cayenne and Kourou use the few beaches when the sun is strongest in the dry season. Few venture far into the sea because the muddy water is uninviting and the currents are strong. Even so there is some windsurfing.

Boating for pleasure is increasingly popular, and on weekends many people take their outboard-motor-powered speedboats to go to the rivers. Some go to explore the miles of mangroves and tiny creeks for fishing or bird-watching, while others use the open spaces for waterskiing.

Chapter 8

THE ECONOMY

The economy of French Guiana is weak and critically underdeveloped in all areas. After years of neglect and misuse of the territory as a penal colony, the French government in 1974 introduced the Green Plan. It was ambitious. It called for a considerable increase in the population, the installation of major timber-processing plants with a view to developing the paper pulp industry, the vitalization of the agricultural industry, and a large-scale road construction project that would open up the interior.

Some of this has been achieved, and bridges have been built across the Mana and the Mahury Rivers, which were previously crossed by ferries. Subsidies have been used to develop the tourist industry and new hotels have been financed. But the plan has not added up to much yet, apart from building. The Cayenne harbor was to be doubled in size and that in Saint-Laurent du Maroni modernized. The commercial port of Cayenne, the Dégrad-des-Cannes, has been built eight miles (thirteen kilometers) from the city on the Mahury River. It handles the major imports and exports. But in most respects the plan has failed to live up to expectations. Reasons given have been lack of planning, corruption, and the difficulty of gaining access to the forest to develop road construction for the timber industry. A crucial factor in French Guiana's lack of economic progress is the shortage of labor, both skilled and unskilled.

Fishing, forestry, and agriculture are the basis of French Guiana's economy. There is very little industry or mining. The department's dependence on France is almost total. The French government spends an estimated $34 million a year in financial and technical aid and on maintaining the space center at Kourou. In 1989 the French government agreed to provide $6 million for a program of economic development to last for five years, with particular emphasis on training, research, job creation, and regional planning.

THE SPACE PROGRAM

The decision to build the space center at Kourou in the early 1960s has been the only significant stimulus to the French Guianese economy. Since 1979 the center has been totally geared to Arianespace, the commercial arm of the European Space Agency based in Paris. Arianespace is responsible for developing the Ariane rockets and selling cargo space on its flights. Its job is to secure orders from organizations, companies, and governments that want to put their satellites into space. Civilian satellites are used principally to record weather patterns, to analyze land use, and in telecommunications. Arianespace currently holds almost 60 percent of the world's commercial launch market, but with the possibility that China, Russia, and even India may soon be competing for business, Arianespace will need to ensure that it retains its customers.

At Kourou there are two launch sites, ELA 1 and ELA 2.

An Ariane rocket is moved to the launch pad.

Between them it is technically possible to deal with up to ten or twelve Ariane launches a year. Since 1980 six versions of the highly successful Ariane 4 rocket launcher have been developed. A new, more powerful rocket, Ariane 5, the "heavy lift" launcher, will offer customers a far greater choice in both the number of satellites per launch and their size. In the first half of the 1990s, more than $17 million per year is being invested in the construction of ELA 3, the new launch facility for the Ariane 5. Ariane rockets are built in Europe and sent by sea from France in sections. The huge containers are unloaded at Dégrad-des-Cannes and then taken under escort on special road transporters to Kourou. The development of the small port at Pariacabo will enable some goods to be transferred from Cayenne by ship.

FISHING AND FORESTRY

Since 1977, French Guiana has owned the fishing rights to a zone stretching for some 200 nautical miles into the Atlantic, covering an area of 50,193 square miles (130,000 square kilometers). The zone is home to a wide variety of fish as well as important reserves of shrimp. In 1992 exports of fishery products amounted to 41 percent of the total export earnings, of which the shrimp catch represented more than half. This was a drop from previous years when, at a peak, shrimp accounted for more than 90 percent of all seafood exports. There is much concern in French Guiana following a ruling made by the European Community (EC) in 1990 that customs barriers on shrimp produced in the poorer countries of South America are to be lowered. This would create considerable competition for the Guianese industry, for which fish is the most important and almost the only export.

With almost 20 million acres (more than 8 million hectares) of forest, timber, particularly hardwoods, are the least exploited of French Guiana's resources. The Guianan forest contains innumerable species of trees, including the *angelique*, a large tree of very hard wood known to come only from French Guiana and bordering forests. Another timber, the wacapou, or brown heart, is closely related to the angelique and used for roof beams. Other valuable timbers include a South American mahogany, which is popular for furniture all over the world, and the Brazilian

Fishing boats at La Larivot on the Cayenne River

rosewood and Saint Martin, both of which are rare woods. Rosewood, with its oil, and mahogany are the major hardwood products. Timber is Guiana's second most-valuable export after fish. There are several sawmills, but projects to increase and improve the industry have been hampered by a lack of infrastructure, such as roads and the high cost of extraction and processing, particularly in the face of lower-cost competition from neighboring Brazil.

MINING

Gold is Guiana's third-largest export commodity. The main industrial sites are at Paul Isnard, Delices, and Changement. There are dredgers on some rivers, but extraction is still underdeveloped. Individual panners work surface deposits such as those at Saint Elie, near Saul in the heart of the forest, from dawn to dusk. Mud and gravel from the gold-bearing deposit are

Gold and rock must be separated.

swirled by hand with a little water in a shallow, conically shaped metal "pan." Gradually the panner eases the lighter material and water over the edge of the pan until just the heavier particles, and—with luck—a few flecks of gold, remain in the bottom of the cone. It is very hard work for a risky return.

Mining of kaolin is beginning in the Mana area on the coast, and substantial deposits of bauxite, silica, niobium, and tantalite have been found, though low market prices and the high cost of development make it difficult to exploit these resources. There is a tile- and brick-manufacturing plant operating near Cayenne, where there are fields of red clay.

AGRICULTURE

Less than 0.2 percent of the total land area is cultivated, and most of what is produced is for the domestic market. Crops are maize (corn), manioc, bananas, and other fruits. The only

The Petit Saut Dam under construction on the Sinnamary River

significant agricultural exports are rice and limes. Rice is grown successfully on *polders*, low-lying land in the region near Mana. A small amount of sugarcane is grown for rum production, but output has declined in recent years.

Cattle raising has always been a problem, so most meat is still imported. Some beef farms have been developed on the coastal plains since the mid-1970s, but the animals suffer from tropical diseases or the climate, which at times is too dry and at times too humid. Other livestock include pigs and poultry.

INDUSTRY AND ENERGY

The manufacturing industry in French Guiana is confined to food processing, in particular shrimp and seafood products, the bottling of a few fruit-flavored colas, the production of yogurt, and rum distillation. There is potential for hydroelectricity, and a dam project, the Petit Saut on the Sinnamary River, is due for completion in 1995. It will supply all the country's needs, including the expansion of the space center at Kourou and the increased demand for energy from a population that has almost trebled since 1977. Until now, French Guiana has relied on imported oil for its energy. The dam will certainly help to cut its import bill.

Construction of the dam, however, has become a controversial environmental issue. Opponents of the dam claim that it will lead to the flooding of 120 square miles (311 square kilometers) of forest. Other protesters claim that the dam will supply far more energy than French Guiana needs.

TOURISM

The tourism sector improved during the 1980s, but it has a long way to go if it is to be a significant part of the economy. There is considerable tourist potential, particularly in the forest with its abundant wildlife and plant life, which are fast disappearing elsewhere on the continent. To a lesser extent the beaches could attract tourists. Although not comparable with beaches in the Caribbean, to date they are not seriously polluted.

Tourists also will be drawn to the decaying remains of the penal colony, most especially in Saint-Laurent du Maroni and on the Iles du Salut. On Ile Royale, the hospital, church, lighthouse, and cemetery still stand and some of the administration houses are being restored. The accommodation once used by the warders has been converted into a hotel. This is popular on weekends with the space technicians and their families. For the less well-off tourist the beaches offer wonderful camping plus all the romance of palms and a tropical island. At present the overgrown and decaying solitary confinement cells on Ile Saint-Joseph are not on the tourist route. Overgrown with twisted lianas and massive roots, they have retained an aura of past horrors.

Chapter 9

THE FUTURE
OF FRENCH GUIANA

TRADING WITH THE WORLD

French Guiana trades with few countries of the world because it is so heavily dependent on France for financial and technical assistance. Approximately half of its imports come from France or the French territories of Martinique and Guadeloupe. The remaining imports come from the United States, Japan, and Germany. The principal imports are food, machinery and transport equipment, petroleum, chemicals, and manufactured goods. Similarly most of its exports—fish, timber, gold, rice, and rum—are sold to France and the French islands, Germany, Japan, and the USA. Exports to the United States consist almost exclusively of shrimp.

The department's import bill far exceeds its export earnings, and since the early 1990s, it has recorded a trade deficit continuously. Its reliance on imported goods also is reflected in the high cost of living, although inflation, which for most of the 1980s averaged around 8 percent, is now much reduced.

Opposite page: Children pose in front of a fountain in the Place Léopold Heder in the old section of Cayenne.

As an overseas department of France, French Guiana automatically belongs to the European Community, which in January 1993 became a single European market, called the European Union (EU). The Guianese fear that this could mean an end to the advantageous trading terms, such as access for exports, which it currently enjoys. A tax on all goods from France and elsewhere, which is vitally necessary to the department's economy, also is to be phased out. However, recognizing the special status of France's overseas departments, the European Union has pledged financial aid specifically to help its economy. The EC acknowledges the special problems of distance from Europe and the need to promote in French Guiana vocational training combined with productive and economic activities.

TRANSPORTATION

One of the main reasons for French Guiana's poor economic record has been its lack of a good transportation system. The only railways in the country have been small local or mining tracks, now disused. A road system is still very limited and is confined largely to the coastal region. Of the more than 600 miles (966 kilometers) of road, about two-thirds are paved. The main route, National Highway 1, runs for just over 150 miles (241 kilometers) between Cayenne and Saint-Laurent du Maroni and was completed in 1976. For the first one hundred years the Cayenne River had to be crossed by a ferry until a bridge was built. This road connects several small towns including Tonate, Macouria, Iracoubo, and, by a branch road and bridge, the agricultural center of Mana.

Eastward from Cayenne there is a paved road for about 100

Newly constructed roads near Cayenne

miles (161 kilometers) to Regina, with a short spur and new bridge to Roura. Another paved spur leads to Cacao. So far there is no paved road to the interior. Without a population to serve or a resource such as a mine, a road would be an expensive luxury.

Water is still a major form of transport, both on the coast and in the interior. Dégrad-des-Cannes is the principal port. Other ports include Le Larivot on the Cayenne River for fishing vessels only; Saint-Laurent, which is used primarily for the export of timber; and Kourou. Jetties and landing slipways exist on the Oyapock and Approuague Rivers. A ferry service crosses the Maroni River between French Guiana and Suriname, though on the Oyapock River only canoes and aluminum speedboats powered by outboard motors make the crossing to Brazil. Canoes still provide the best means of access to the interior, because large vessels are prevented from going upstream by the numerous rapids.

Passengers boarding an Air Guyane plane at Rochambeau International Airport

The arrival of air transport in the twentieth century has helped open up the interior, and the local airline, Air Guyane, has regular flights with small aircraft to Saul, Maripasoula on the Maroni River, Regina on the Approuague River, and Saint-Georges on the Oyapock River. Light aircraft can be hired and will land on locally made strips in the jungle. Rochambeau International Airport, eleven miles (eighteen kilometers) from Cayenne, is equipped to handle large jet aircraft, and there are international flights to and from France, Suriname, and Brazil. Plans have been made for its development.

COMMUNICATION

The main newspaper is the daily *France-Guyane*, published in Cayenne but printed in Guadeloupe. Much of its coverage is of local interest, but there is international and French news, with some pages devoted to French soccer and racing results. French theater, books, and films get lengthy reviews in a Saturday supplement, along with the week's local television and news of TV personalities. Other newspapers are small and include *La Presse Guyane,* of which only a thousand copies are published. Some international newspapers and magazines also are available, particularly from France and Brazil.

Radio-Télévision Française d'Oûtre-mer (RFO) has two television channels and broadcasts in French or shows films from the United States and Europe with subtitles. Local news and affairs are added to the program schedule. Broadcasting normally begins at midday and runs until midnight. There are an estimated 22,000 television receivers in the country. Satellite receivers are common and Brazilian television is always available. There are several independent radio stations, including Cayenne FM and Radio Antipa, which broadcasts in Creole and Boni.

The telephone service is run by France Telecom and reaches all but the most distant villages, where radiotelephones still are used. Even these are gradually being replaced by modern satellite equipment, and it is possible to call the world from public phone booths standing beside a jungle river.

THE FUTURE

Few countries in the world, if any, have had such a bizarre history as that of French Guiana. First it was a land that nobody wanted to know until rumors of gold spread, next it became a colony whose economy was based entirely on a slave population imported from Africa, then for almost one hundred years it was a penal colony. This constitutes many years in which little was done to develop the country. Now, toward the end of the twentieth century, it is a country of paradox. French Guiana is one of the most underdeveloped lands in the Americas. Yet it is the setting for one of the major technological achievements of the twentieth century.

Only in the past fifty years or so has French Guiana been able to think for itself about what its future might be. Under France's constitution of 1946 it was confirmed that all citizens of the overseas departments had rights equal to the French living in France. While this may seem to be true in terms of voting rights and representation in the French parliament, many Guianese have yet to be convinced that it is so in their everyday lives. A few voices have already been heard calling for independence, but for the time being they have been silenced mainly by the inflow of funds from France. The majority of the population, while not wanting full independence, does seem to favor a measure of autonomy or the right to make certain decisions for themselves. But any movement toward independence must surely be based on the ability of the country to be economically independent. It is difficult to see how that might be achieved in French Guiana, for although the forest covering so much of the country may be rich in timber, the difficulty and cost of exploitation might well prove prohibitive.

In the meantime France continues to fund the overseas department. But some warning shots have been fired. Speaking early in 1990, then French Prime Minister Michel Rocard said that the chapter on colonialism was closing for the overseas departments, and that the future for French Guiana should now lie in developing cultural, economic, and financial linkages with the Caribbean, to which the country belongs geographically but into which it has never been fully integrated.

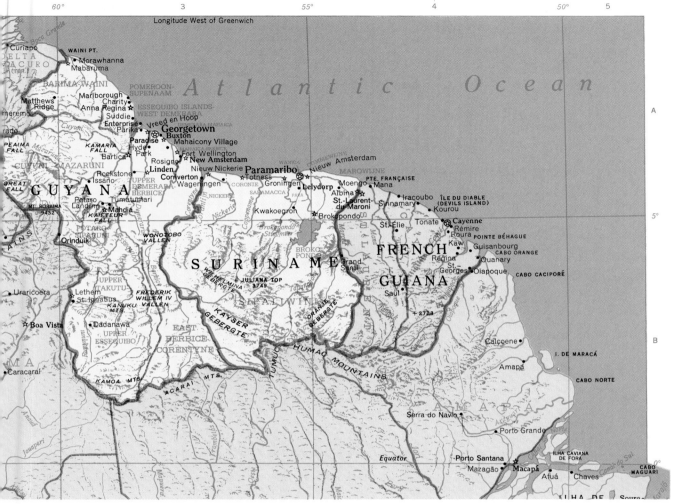

MAP KEY

Camopi, *river*	B4	Oyapock, *river*	B4
Cayenne	B4	Pointe Béhague, *cape*	B4
Cayenne, *territory*	A4, B4	Pointe Française, *cape*	A4
Comté, *river*	B4	Regina	B4
Grand Santi	B4	Rémire	B4
Guisanbourg	B4	Roura	B4
Ile Du Diable (Devil's Island)	A4	Saül	B4
Iracoubo	A4	Sinnamary	A4
Kaw	B4	St. Élie	B4
Kourou	A4	St.-Georges	B4
Mana	A4	St. Laurent, *territory*	A4, B4
Mana, *river*	A4, B4	St.-Laurent-du-Maroni	A4
Maroni, *river*	A4, B4	Tampok, *river*	B4
Ouanary	B4	Tonate	B4

MINI-FACTS AT A GLANCE

GENERAL INFORMATION

Official Name: *Departemente de la Guyane Francaise* (Department of French Guiana)

Capital: Cayenne

Government: French Guiana is an overseas department of France with additional status as a Region of France; it has an economic and political status similar to that of any department in France. French Guiana sends two elected deputies to the French National Assembly and one elected representative to the French Senate in Paris. The president of France is the chief of state. French Guiana also is represented at the European Parliament in Strasbourg.
  The administration is headed by a prefect (governor) appointed by France. There are two legislative houses, General Council and Regional Council. French Guiana is divided into two *arrondissements* (administrative units), Cayenne and Saint-Laurent du Maroni.

Religion: There is no official religion in French Guiana, but the majority of people follow Christianity. The largest religious group is the Roman Catholics (85 percent); followed by Protestants, 4 percent; and others, 11 percent. Buddhism and Islam are practiced among the East Indians and Southeast Asians. The Indians follow their own spiritual beliefs.

Ethnic Composition: The largest group of people is Creoles (a mix of black and white races). Amerindians are distributed into six major tribes: Arawak, Emerillon, Galibi, Oyampi, Palikur, and Wayana. Lebanese, Chinese, Moroccans, Laotians, Haitians, Brazilians, Vietnamese, and people from the French Caribbean islands make up most of the immigrant population.

Language: The official language is French. Almost everyone understands and speaks French; it is also the medium of instruction in schools. Maroon Indians have their own language, Taki-Taki, a mixture of African dialects, English, and Dutch. The Creole dialect is an assortment of African and French mixed with some Portuguese and English words.

National Flag: The French tricolor of red, white, and blue is the official flag of French Guiana.

Money: In March 1996 one French franc was worth $0.1980 in United States currency.

Membership in International Organizations: European Union (EU); World Federation of Trade Unions (WFTU)

Weights and Measures: The metric system is in use.

Population: In 1995 the population was 145,270; 3.6 persons per sq. mi. (1.4 persons per sq km); 82 percent urban, 18 percent rural

Cities:

Cayenne	41,164
Kourou	13,848
Saint-Laurent du Maroni	13,606
Remire-Montjoly	11,709
Matoury	10,131

(Population is based on the 1990 census.)

GEOGRAPHY

Border: French Guiana lies on the north coast of South America near the equator. The Atlantic Ocean is to the north, Brazil is to the east and south, and Suriname is to the west.

Coastline: The Atlantic coastline extends for about 200 mi. (320 km). Offshore rocky islands of Iles du Salut are part of French Guiana; these islands were the base of French prison camps in the early 20th century.

Land: There are three main land regions in French Guiana: a low swampy coastal plain extending for about 200 mi. (320 km) in the north; a grassy plateau extending for about 50 mi. (80 km) in the center; and the Tumuc-Humac Mountains and other low hilly ranges in the south, forming the border with Brazil. Large swamps exist in the coastal areas, especially along the river mouths. The Swamp of Kaw is the largest swamp covering 250,000 acres (101,173 hectares) southeast of Cayenne. The swamps are noted for their wildlife, particularly reptiles and birds.

Highest Point: 2,723 ft. (830 m)

Lowest Point: Sea level

Rivers: The River Maroni is the longest river in French Guiana and is known as the Litani River in some parts. The Oyapock, Mana, and Sinnamary are other major rivers. Heavy sediment deposited by rivers form mud banks as long as 25 mi. (40 km) along the coast. Few rivers are navigable by small boats for more than 60 mi. (97 km) from the mouth. Bridges have been constructed recently over certain parts of the Mana and Mahury Rivers where previously ferries were used to cross the rivers.

Forests: Some 90 percent of the country is covered by tropical rain forests. Giant trees reach heights of 120 ft (37 m). The rosewood and mahogany are the major hardwood products. Palms of many kinds are common and are a valuable source for oils, wood, leaves for thatch, and fibers for many uses. The *tabebuias* is an extremely hardwood tree, much in demand for export. The ceiba tree produces an abundance of kapok (a cottonlike fiber). French Guiana has an immense variety of flowering trees and shrubs. Orchids with delicate flowers are numerous. Philodendrons, bromeliads, red annattoes, and water hyacinths are in abundance.

Wildlife: The tropical fauna includes common opossums, cougars, skunks, armadillos, monkeys, deer, giant otters, tapirs, wild pigs, jaguars, and ocelots. Butterflies, beetles, and spiders abound in the rain forests. Reptiles include crocodiles, snakes, and iguana lizards. The maritime turtles return annually to nest on the sandy beaches of Les Hattes. The forestry service and the World Wide Fund for Nature monitor the protection of the giant leatherback turtles during their nesting season.

French Guiana is the home to many tropical bird species, including scarlet ibis, macaws, parrots, bellbirds, woodpeckers, hummingbirds, egrets, herons, storks, eagles, and vultures.

Climate: The tropical climate has almost constantly high daytime temperatures of 79° F (26° C). Rainfall is heavy throughout the year and averages about 130 in. (330 cm) annually. The rainy season extends from November to July. The average humidity throughout the year is 85 percent.

Greatest Distance: North to South: 250 mi. (400 km)
East to West: 190 mi. (300 km)

Area: 35,135 sq. mi. (91,000 sq km)

ECONOMY AND INDUSTRY

Agriculture: Less than 0.2 percent of the total land is under cultivation. Crops include maize (corn), rice, manioc, bananas, limes, pineapples, yams, sugarcane, and some other fruits. Most small farms are worked and owned by families, but there are a few large estates growing chiefly commercial crops. Since agriculture is very limited, most of the food must be imported from overseas. Tropical diseases have hindered the growth of livestock; some pigs and poultry are raised in rural areas.

Fishing: French Guiana has fishing rights to a zone of 200 nautical miles in the Atlantic Ocean. This area is an excellent reserve of a wide variety of fish and shrimp. An abundance of piranhas, electric eels, sting rays, pacus, coumarous, small sharks, red snappers, and shrimp are found in the inland waters and in the ocean.

Mining: There are small deposits of gold, bauxite, and kaolin. Kaolin mining is concentrated in the Mana area. Substantial deposits of silica, niobium, and tantalite have been found, but processing is difficult because of the inaccessibility of interior areas. Energy is derived chiefly from petroleum.

Manufacturing: French Guiana has a very small manufacturing industry. There are a few sawmills, but enlargement of the timber industry is difficult because of a lack of infrastructure of roads and processing plants. There is a tile and brick plant near Cayenne. Other manufacturing plants include food processing (shrimp and seafood), bottling of a few fruit-flavored colas, and rum distillation.

Space Program: The town of Kourou on the Atlantic Coast has been developed as the Guianese Space Center, or Europe's Spaceport, from which commercial Ariane rockets and satellites are launched. Since 1979 the Kourou center has been totally geared to Arianespace, the commercial arm of the European Space Agency based in Paris. Largely expanded in the 1990s, the Space Center continues to provide a stimulus to the economy. In 1991 some 1,100 people were employed there.

Transportation: The transportation infrastructure is not well developed. There are no railroads in use at present. The road system is very limited and confined largely to the coastal areas. The main highway runs for about 150 mi. (240 km) between Cayenne and Saint-Laurent du Maroni. There are no paved roads in the interior. In the early 1990s, there were some 25,000 passenger cars and 9,000 commercial vehicles in use. A daily hydrofoil takes visitors from Kourou to the Iles du Salut. Ferries cross the Maroni River between French Guiana and Suriname. Canoes still provide the best means of access to the interior. Outboard motors transport goods—oil, rice, alcohol, cigarettes, fruit, coconuts, and even some gold—across some major rivers. Air Guyane is the local airline with regular flights to cities within French Guiana. Rochambeau International Airport near Cayenne is equipped to handle large aircraft. In 1991 there were 8 airports with scheduled flights. The commercial port of Cayenne, handling major imports and exports of French Guiana, is built 8 mi. (13 km) from the city on the Mahury River.

Communication: The daily *France-Guyane* is the main newspaper. French Guiana has two television channels; easy availability of satellite receivers has made Brazilian television very popular. Telephone service covers all but some remote villages. In the early 1990s there was one radio receiver per 1.5 persons, one television set per 6 persons, and one telephone per 3.9 persons.

Trade: The chief imports are food, machinery and transport equipment, petroleum, chemicals, and manufactured goods. About half of French Guiana's imports come from France or the French territories of Martinique and Guadeloupe; other imports come from the United States, Japan, and Germany. The chief export items are fish and shrimp, wood and cork, gold, rice, and rum. Major export destinations are France and the French islands, Germany, Japan, and the United States.

EVERYDAY LIFE

Health: The Institut Pasteur at Cayenne is well known in Latin America; it undertakes research into diseases such as yellow fever, tuberculosis, leprosy, and malaria. Improvement in medical care has led to a decline in the death rate and an increase in the birth rate. In the 1980s life expectancy for males was 63 years and for females 70 years. The infant mortality rate at 23 per 1,000 is high. In the late 1980s there were 375 persons per physician and 103 persons per hospital bed. Most of the health care facilities are concentrated in Cayenne.

Education: Education is free and compulsory and is modeled after the French system. Primary school starts at the age of six and continues for five years, and secondary level starts at the age of eleven and lasts for up to seven years. The Lycée Vidal in Cayenne is a modern school that offers students many possible educational facilities. Mathematics, economics, history, and geography are taught in schools. In Indian territories some schools have been established with teachers who are contracted from France. Higher education is provided by universities in France or at a branch of the University Antilles-Guyane in Cayenne. Technical studies, teacher-training, and agricultural studies are offered in other colleges. In the early 1990s the literacy rate was about 82 percent.

Holidays:
New Year's Day, January 1
Labor Day, May 1
National Day, July 14
Armistice Day, November 11
Christmas, December 25
Some Buddhist, Christian, and Muslim holiday celebrations vary every year, depending on the calendars used by the groups. Even the Carnival in Cayenne occurs on a different date each year.

Society: In some Indian societies the women tend the gardens and grow manioc, yams, sweet potatoes, and bananas while the men fish, hunt, and clear the forest for planting. Most of the handicrafts are based on wood from local forests; these include decorative bowls, containers, cups, animal shapes, baskets, bows, arrows, seed and bead necklaces, clay pottery, and chairs. Many different-colored woods are sometimes used to make an object and then it is polished very fine by hand. Hmong people make beautiful red-and-black embroidered cloth. Glass-framed pictures made with colorful butterfly wings also are popular.

Dress: Most of the urban population wears Western-style clothing. Some Indian groups also wear Western clothes, including shorts and T-shirts. Some Indians wear a wraparound skirt and occasionally they paint their bodies.

Housing: Most houses are constructed of wood and have iron roofs. The government has been constructing modern three- or four-story apartment buildings, bungalows, and small houses of many kinds in urban areas. In older sections of towns three- and four-story timber buildings and multi-colored shops and houses are a common sight. Most of the homes on the coast have running water and electricity. Wayana Indians on the coast sometimes live in thatch and wood huts with a roof. To aid ventilation, there are no walls. In these huts, hammocks are the main piece of furniture.

Food: Local food is influenced by French, Chinese, and Asian styles. Most of the canned food is flown in once or twice a week from France. Creole cooking uses rice, yams, breadfruit, and manioc; it is spiced with green lemons, peppers, nutmeg, and cayenne pepper. A variety of fish and game from the forest forms part of the daily diet. Shark poached in wine and lemon juice and cooked with onions, spices, and whole chilies is a popular dish. From manioc flour a large biscuit-thin cake is made and dried in the sun. It is then eaten with soups and meat. Coca-cola and French wines are popular drinks. Cashiri is a popular drink made by boiling manioc and allowing it to ferment.

Sports and Recreation: Soccer is popular everywhere in French Guiana, even in some Indian communities. Cycling, *boules* (a game played with heavy metal balls), some boating, fishing, bird-watching, and windsurfing also are enjoyed. Some European dances such as the waltz and the mazurka are popular, but there is very little local dance or music. The best-known music is reggae. Brazilian music is often played on the radio. The biggest festival in French Guiana is the Carnival in Cayenne.

Social Welfare: The system of social security is similar to France. It provides payments for work injury, unemployment, and maternity.

IMPORTANT DATES

1500—Two explorers land for the first time on the coast of present-day French Guiana

1543—The Viceroyalty of Peru, governed from Spain, is established

1595—Sir Robert Dudley sends a crew up the Orinoco River; Sir Walter Raleigh arrives in French Guiana

1597-98—The first Dutch expedition arrives on the Guiana coast

1602—Henri IV of France gives permission to create a Guiana colony

1616—Raleigh returns to Guianas for further explorations; the Dutch establish a trading post on the Essequibo River in present-day Guyana

1621—The Dutch West Indian Company is created

1643—A French commercial company called the Cape North Company is formed in Rouen, France; the original settlement of present-day Cayenne is founded

1652—Another French commercial company is formed

1664—The first permanent French colony is established

1667—The Treaty of Breda awards the French Guiana territory to France

1678—The French recover Cayenne from the Dutch

1762—The Jesuits, who had arrived in the previous century, are expelled from Guiana territory

1776—French governor Victor Malouet arrives in Guiana

1777—The Canal Laussant is built

1788—The rebel leader Aluku Nenge dit Boni is captured and beheaded

1793—A decree abolishes slavery in Cayenne

1802—French authorities permit the reintroduction of slavery

1809—Cayenne is taken over by Portugal

1814—Cayenne is returned to France

1827—Mother Javouhey arrives in French Guiana

1848—Slavery is finally and officially abolished in French Guiana; people get full French citizenship and the right to vote

1851—Sugar production drops to about 885,000 pounds (401,000 kilograms) from 5 million pounds (2.2 million kilograms) in 1847

1852—Emperor Napoleon III of France decides to send more manpower in the form of convicts to French Guiana

1854—The French Guiana colony is governed by a senate decree of Napoleon III; a formal prison colony is established in French Guiana

1857—All French colonies, including French Guiana, become French Departments; the Gold and Agricultural Company of the River Approuague is created

1901—The last gold rush occurs in the Inini and Haute-Mana regions

1919—Jean Galmont is elected a deputy to the French Assembly

1931—French lawyer G. Monnerville is elected a deputy to the French Assembly

1938—The French National Assembly votes to abolish the penal colony in French Guiana

1946—French Guiana becomes La Guyane, an overseas department of France

1954—The last convict from the prison camps is returned to France

1964—The French government chooses the site of Kourou for its space program

1974—French Guiana is granted regional status by France; France introduces the Green Plan (*Plan Vert*) to boost French Guiana's economy

1976—National Highway 1 is completed

1977—A group of 500 Hmongs from Laos arrives and settles in the village of Cacao

1980—A number of bomb attacks against "colonial" and government targets occur

1986—Suriname's civil war sends thousands of refugees to French Guiana

1987—French Premier Jacques Chirac visits Kourou; a second group of Hmongs arrives and settles near Saint-Laurent du Maroni

1989—French troops are brought in to patrol borders with Suriname; *Phèdre Plan* is launched with the aim of spreading Kourou's wealth throughout French Guiana

1991—A strike called for preventing the launch of a rocket is unsuccessful; exports of fish amount to some 60 percent of the total exports; a strike by the local political parties forces France to withdraw from a deal with South Africa to explore gold deposits in French Guiana

1992—Regional council elections are held; almost all of the 5,900 Suriname refugees accept financial incentives from the French administration to leave French Guiana and return to Suriname

1993—The European Community (EC), now European Union (EU), becomes a single European market

1995—The space launching station at Kourou is honored on a French stamp

IMPORTANT PEOPLE

Antoine Lefébure de la Barre, a French diplomat; laid the foundation of the first permanent French settlement in French Guiana

Antonio de Berrío, Spanish explorer

Leonard Berry, one of Walter Raleigh's lieutenants; sent to explore the rivers of the Guianas in 1596

Poncet de Brétigny, Frenchman who in 1643 established a small settlement near Ceperou Hill with three hundred Frenchmen

Andre Cognat, Frenchman who is a spokesperson for the rights of Wayana Indian people

Jean-Francois Cordet, Prefect of French Guiana in 1993

León Damas (1912-   ), literary figure; led the Caribbean *modernismo* movement in the 1920s

Captain Alfred Dreyfus (c. 1859-1935), one of the French inhabitants of the Iles du Salut prison camp

Sir Robert Dudley (1573-1649), the first Englishman to send a crew to present-day French Guiana

Jean Galmont, French businessman; elected a deputy to the French Assembly from French Guiana

Mother Superior Anne-Marie Javouhey (1779-1851), one of the "saints" of French Guiana; established missions for freed slaves and a leper hospital with assistance from Father Libermann

Lawrence Keymis, English explorer; accompanied Walter Raleigh on expeditions in French Guiana

Jean-Paul and Françoise Klingelhofer, French couple who have lived with the Wayana Indians for twenty years; they teach in school and run a dispensary in the village of Twenke; they also started *Culture Artisat Wayana* (CAWAY), a handicraft cooperative

Albert Londres (1884-1932), French journalist who exposed the truth behind the penal colony of French Guiana

Alonso de Ojeda (1465-1515), Spanish explorer of the northern coast of South America

Sir Walter Raleigh (1554-1618), an English explorer, navigator, and historian; wrote *Discoveries of the large, rich and beautiful Empire of Guiana, with a relation of the great and golden citie of Manoa (which the Spaniards call El Dorado)* in 1596

Amerigo Vespucci (1454-1512), Italian explorer

Compiled by Chandrika Kaul

INDEX

Page numbers that appear in boldface type indicate illustrations

Newly graduated with a degree in history from the University of Wales, Marion Morrison first traveled to South America in 1962 with a British volunteer program to work among Aymara Indians living near Lake Titicaca. In Bolivia she met her husband, British filmmaker and writer Tony Morrison. In the last twenty-five years the Morrisons, who make their home in England, have visited almost every country of South and Central America, making television documentary films, photographing, and researching—sometimes accompanied by their children, Kimball and Rebecca.

Marion Morrison has written about South American countries for Macmillan's Let's Visit series, and for Wayland Publisher's Peoples, How They Lived and Life and Times series. Mrs. Morrison also has written *Bolivia, Columbia, Paraguay, Uruguay,* and *Venezuela* in the Enchantment of the World series. Resulting from their travels, the Morrisons have created their South American Picture Library that contains more than seventy-five thousand pictures of the continent.

And ther .2. dougter, one, all liuing
and other of their children mari
ageds. So .15. are come of them.

2

Mr Brewster liued to very old
age; about .80. yeers. he was when he
dyed, hauing liued some .23. or
.24. years here in y countrie. (3
though his wife dyed long before,
yet she dyed aged. His sone Wras-
tle dyed a yonge man vnmaried,
his sone Loue liued till this year .1650.
and dyed & left .4. children, now
liuing. His doughters which came
over after him, are dead. But haue
left sundry children aliue; his
eldest sone is still liueing, and
hath .9. or .10. children, one maried who hath a child, or .2.

4

Richard more, his brother dyed the
first winter; but he is maried, and
hath .4. or .5. children, all liuing.

Mr Ed: Winslow, his wife dyed the
first winter; and he maried with
the widow of mr White, and hath .2.
children liuing by her mariagable,
besids sundry that are dead.
one of his seruants dyed, as also the
litle girles soone after the ships a-
riual. But his man Georg Sowle
is still liuing, and hath .8. childr

William Bradford, his wife dyed
soone after their ariual; and he
maried againe; and hath .4. children .3. wherof are maried. _ _ _
who dyed 9 of May .1655.

4

Mr Allerton his wife dyed with the
first, and his seruant John Hooke.
his sone Bartle is maried in England
but y know not how many children
he hath. His doughter remember is
maried at Salem & hath .3. or .4

8

Mr fuller, his seruant dyed at sea; and
after his wife came over, he had tow
children by her; which are liuing
and growne vp to yers. But he dyed
some .15. years agoe.

2

John Crakston dyed in the first mortality; and about some .5. or .6. years
after his sone dyed, hauing lost him
selfe in y woods, his feet became frosen,
which put him into a feauor, of which
he dyed.

8

Captain Standish his wife dyed in
the first sicknes; and he maried
againe, and hath .4. sones liueing, and some are dead.
→ who dyed .3. of octob. 1655.

4

Mr Martin, he and all his, dyed
in the first ynfection; not long
after the ariual.

Mr Molines, and his wife, his
sone, & his seruant dyed the first
winter. only his dougter priscila
suruied, and maried with John
Alden, who are both liuing, and
haue .11. children. And their eldest
daughter is maried & hath fiue
children. See N. E. Memorial.
p. 22.

15

Mr White, and his .2. seruants dyed
soone after ther landing. His wife maried with mr Winslow (as is before noted)
His .2. sons are maried, and resolued
hath .5. children; perigrine too,
all liuing. so their yncrease are 7

7

Mr Hopkins, and his wife are now
both dead; But they liued aboue

---

his d---------------- ma-
ried. a---------------- of
them liuing, and one of them ma-
reed

Mr Richard Warren liued some .4.
or .5. years, and had his wife come
over to him, by whom he had .2.
sons before dyed; and one of them
is maryed, and hath .2. children
so his yncrease is .4. But he had
.5. doughters more came over
with his wife, who are all maried, & liuing & haue many children.

4

John Billinton after he had bene
here .10. yers, was executed, for
killing a man; and his eldest
sone dyed before him; But his
.2. sone is aliue, and maried, &
hath .8. children

8

Edward Tillie, and his wife both
dyed soon after their ariual; and
the girle Humility their cousen was
sent for into Ento England, and
dyed ther. But the youth Henry
samson, is still liueing, and is
maried, & hath .7. children.

7

John Tillie, and his wife both
dyed, a litle after they came
a shore; and their daughter Elizabeth maried with John Howland and hath ysue as is before noted.

Francis Cooke is still liuing a

LOS PEREGRINOS DE N. C. WYETH

A los educadores de América—

Todos los amigos que he conocido y que aún me quedan

por conocer, y que cada día mantienen vivo en las aulas

el sueño de los Peregrinos, desde Plymouth hasta Pago Pago.

El autor y el editor agradecen profundamente a la Plantación de Plimouth su entusiasta y valiosa colaboración en la preparación del texto de este libro, y a la compañía de seguros *Metropolitan Life*, en particular al señor Stephen Loesch, que hicieron posible la publicación de este libro.

LOS PEREGRINOS DE N.C. WYETH
Traducción de Alberto Romo

Spanish translation copyright © 1992 by Lectorum Publications, Inc.
Originally published in English under the title
N.C. Wyeth's Pilgrims
Illustrations courtesy of Metropolitan Life Insurance Company
Photographer: Malcom Varon
Text copyright © 1991 by Robert San Souci.
Illustrations copyright © 1945 by Metropolitan Life Insurance Company

The endpapers of this book are copies of the Mayflower's original passenger list, courtesy of the Plimouth Plantation.
Book design by Kathy Warinner

This edition published by arrangement with the original Publisher
Chronicle Books, San Francisco, California, USA

ISBN 1-880507-03-X

Printed in Hong Kong

Published by:
Lectorum Publications, Inc.
137 West 14th Street
New York, NY 10011

LOS PEREGRINOS DE N.C. WYETH

TEXTO DE ROBERT SAN SOUCI
LECTORUM PUBLICATIONS, NEW YORK

os siglos XVI y XVII fueron épocas de persecuciones religiosas en Inglaterra. Los gobernantes querían que sus súbditos solamente siguieran el mandato de la iglesia oficial, pero algunas personas tenían diferentes creencias. Uno de esos grupos, llamado "Separatistas", realizaba reuniones secretas, pero se atemorizaron cuando algunos de sus miembros fueron encarcelados. Ellos se marcharon de Inglaterra hacia Holanda pero no lograron adaptarse a vivir allí. Al correr el tiempo, tuvieron noticias de una colonia en Norteamérica, llamada Virginia. Este Nuevo Mundo prometía tierras, oportunidades económicas, y lo más importante: la esperanza de poder practicar su religión con libertad. Fue así como los Separatistas decidieron hacer la travesía por mar y establecer su propia colonia en Norteamérica.

Llegaron a un acuerdo con un grupo de hombres de negocios de Londres: los colonizadores recibirían el pasaje y provisiones y, en cambio, ellos enviarían a la Compañía Londinense, pescado, pieles y madera durante siete años. Los Separatistas de Holanda compraron un barco, el *Speedwell*. Los de Londres contrataron otra nave, el *Mayflower*. Aun con dos barcos, muchos de los Separatistas tuvieron que quedarse en Europa, con la esperanza de poder hacer el viaje más adelante.

Ambas naves zarparon del puerto de Southampton, Inglaterra, pero en dos ocasiones el *Speedwell* sufrió averías que le obligaron a regresar, seguido por el *Mayflower*. Finalmente, el día 6 de septiembre de 1620, el *Mayflower* partió solo de Plymouth, Inglaterra, en su histórico viaje.

Aunque no existen retratos del *Mayflower*, los investigadores han logrado reconstruir su apariencia por medio de documentos y pinturas de esa época. Probablemente era una embarcación de tres mástiles, noventa pies de largo y con una tripulación de veinticinco marineros.

De los ciento dos pasajeros que viajaban amontonados en las estancias de popa, cuarenta y cuatro (19 hombres, 11 mujeres y 14 niños) eran Separatistas; el resto había sido reclutado por la Compañía Londinense. Considerados por los Separatistas como "extranjeros", ellos no compartían totalmente las creencias religiosas de éstos, pero igualmente anhelaban la oportunidad de comenzar una nueva vida. Entre ellos se encontraba Myles Standish, un soldado profesional que había sido contratado como comandante de la milicia de los Separatistas. También viajaban en el barco gallinas, cabras y dos perros.

El ruido era un constante compañero de viaje: el crujir de la madera, el choque entre velas y aparejos, el fluir del agua por el casco y el roer de las ratas. De noche, alrededor de noventa personas dormían en un área conocida como "entre puentes"; la mayoría de ellos en colchones de paja sobre el duro suelo. La ventilación era mala, y el poco espacio que había estaba ocupado con barriles de provisiones, arcas y materiales de construcción. No había un solo lugar a bordo donde encontrar silencio y tranquilidad.

Las tensiones entre la tripulación y los pasajeros aumentaron. A la tripulación le molestaban los cantos de los salmos y las oraciones diarias de los Separatistas, mientras que a los peregrinos les disgustaban las blasfemias de los marineros.

El vaivén y movimiento de las olas convirtió el mareo en un problema constante. Para aquellos pasajeros que podían comer, la mayoría de las comidas era muy sencilla: carne o pescado salado, galletas duras y secas. También había guisantes, habas, frutas secas, queso y mantequilla. Para beber sólo tenían cerveza, que bebían incluso los niños. El aburrimiento, la nostalgia, la falta de higiene, y el miedo contribuían a que se sintieran desesperados. Durante el viaje, uno de los asistentes del médico de a bordo murió de fiebre y fue sepultado en el mar. A un niño que nació durante la travesía lo bautizaron con el nombre de "Océano".

El tiempo era muy variable: unas veces calmado y benigno, y otras veces se desataban grandes tormentas. Durante una de esas

tormentas, la viga principal del barco se partió. Algunos pensaron que era el fin, pero el barco logró resistir la tormenta, y la viga fue reparada con un cilindro de hierro que habían transportado para la construcción de viviendas. Durante el transcurso de otra tormenta, un pasajero cayó al mar pero logró sujetarse de una cuerda que colgaba del barco y pudo ser rescatado.

Fue así como algunos de los pasajeros oyeron los primeros gritos de "Tierra" y se amontonaron en los pasillos para mirar la tierra que sería su hogar. Habían estado en el mar durante 66 días, pero el 11 de noviembre de 1620 llegaban a su destino tras un intrépido y arriesgado viaje. En realidad, el destino les tenía reservado muchas más aventuras y peligros.

D esde la cubierta del barco, los pasajeros contemplaron un paisaje desolador. Algunos de los marineros comentaron que el lugar estaba lleno de animales y de hombres salvajes, llamados "Indios". Varios pasajeros pensaron regresar a Inglaterra, pero la mayoría estaba decidida a quedarse y comenzaron a trazar planes.

Como habían desembarcado lejos del lugar a donde se dirigían originalmente, que era Virginia, los "extranjeros" pensaron que no tenían que cumplir con el convenio hecho con los comerciantes de Londres. Pero los Separatistas argumentaron que deberían proceder según lo pactado. Finalmente, estuvieron de acuerdo y juntos redactaron un convenio conocido como el "Pacto de Mayflower", que sentó los principios que gobernarían la nueva colonia. Desde ese momento, se mezclaron de tal forma que a todos se les ha llegado a conocer con el nombre de "Peregrinos".

Los primeros en salir a explorar la tierra abandonaron el barco el 11 de noviembre. Reabastecieron sus escasas provisiones de agua y comida y se adentraron en la tierra, maravillándose de la abundancia que encontraban a su paso. El lunes 13 de noviembre, hicieron un desembarco para reparar la chalupa (una pequeña embarcación que utilizaban para realizar exploraciones). Mientras los hombres la repararon, las mujeres lavaron las ropas. Debido a que durante la travesía solamente habían podido enjuagarlas en agua salada, demoraron todo un día en realizar esta labor. Tendidas para airearse, las ropas parecían un verdadero arco iris: faldas rojas, pantalones azules, capas púrpuras y medias de color verde.

Al poco tiempo salió una segunda expedición. En esta ocasión hallaron los restos de una cabaña con extraños montículos cercanos. Excavando la tierra, los exploradores encontraron cestos llenos de maíz. Ellos llamaron a este lugar la "Colina de Maíz" y trajeron cuarenta fanegas al barco, prometiéndose que pagarían por ellas más tarde, lo cual hicieron. Para los peregrinos, a bordo del *Mayflower*, el maíz multicolor debe haberles parecido, sin duda alguna, un signo de buena suerte. Con suficientes semillas para plantar en la primavera, la esperanza renacía para ellos.

Pero los vientos gélidos del invierno y la lluvia helada pronto consiguieron que todos tomaran refugio bajo cubierta, excepto los marineros más acostumbrados a las inclemencias del tiempo. Los hombres que regresaban de tierra decían que ésta estaba cubierta de nieve. La necesidad de encontrar un lugar para asentar su colonia se hizo más urgente. Para muchos la situación les debió parecer no mejor que cuando estaban en alta mar. Ellos se preguntaban si encontrarían alguna vez el lugar adecuado para establecer su hogar.

Salieron nuevas expediciones, incluyendo una que se aventuró lejos en la chalupa, a mediados de diciembre. Una noche, durante este viaje, mientras acampaban en la orilla, oyeron un grito extraño. Aterrorizados y confusos, los hombres dispararon sus mosquetes en todas direcciones hasta que el ruido cesó. Ellos se convencieron a sí mismos que sólo habían escuchado el aullido de los lobos, pero no lograron conciliar el sueño esa noche.

A la mañana siguiente, temprano, oyeron el grito nuevamente. Los peregrinos dispararon dos veces y se retiraron. Los indios, a cierta distancia, continuaban sus gritos. Aunque lanzaron muchas flechas contra la barricada, milagrosamente nadie resultó herido, ni entre los indios, ni entre los peregrinos. Éstos recogieron las flechas, las que posteriormente enviaron a Inglaterra como "curiosidades", y continuaron sus exploraciones. Los peregrinos llamaron a este lugar: "Primer Encuentro".

El viernes 9 de diciembre, los peregrinos descubrieron una pequeña cala. El lunes siguiente, exploraron las aguas para ver si eran lo suficientemente profundas para que pudieran atracar barcos grandes. Amarraron la chalupa y bajaron a explorar tierra adentro. Encontraron campos de maíz abandonados, y bosques que proporcionarían suficiente madera, así como corrientes de agua fresca. Por fin habían llegado al lugar que estaban buscando.

Los peregrinos permane-
cieron gran parte de ese
primer invierno a bordo
del *Mayflower*. Solamente
tenían dos pequeñas embarcaciones, y el mal
tiempo demoraba el desembarco. Mientras
que algunos descargaban las provisiones,
otros se dedicaban a construir pequeñas
cabañas y una casa común que serviría de
vivienda para la mayoría de ellos y para alma-
cenar las provisiones. Un fuego destruyó el
techo de la casa común, lo que atrasó más el
trabajo. Como no podían perder sus provisiones, todos trabajaron afanosamente hasta
salvarlas, pero no pudieron continuar las
reparaciones debido a los estragos causados
por las enfermedades.

La más temible de todas era la pulmonía, aunque en aquella época pensaban que era escorbuto, ocasionada por la falta de refugio adecuado, y por las frías temperaturas del agua al pasar de la chalupa a tierra. Al llegar abril, la mitad de los peregrinos había fallecido—a veces, dos o tres en el mismo día. Un reducido número, incluyendo al Capitán Myles Standish, se mantuvo en buen estado de salud, y a pesar de sus incansables esfuerzos por ayudar a los otros, continuaron las pérdidas humanas. Debido a su pequeño número, los peregrinos temían ser atacados por los indios, pero éstos se mantenían a distancia. En una ocasión se apoderaron de unas herramientas que encontraron abandonadas, pero generalmente huian si un peregrino se les acercaba.

A mediados de marzo, un guerrero indio entró en el campamento de Plymouth. Hablaba un inglés muy peculiar, difícil de entender, pero los peregrinos averiguaron que su nombre era Samoset. Él era un *Abnaki sagamore* o un jefe, de lo que hoy es Maine. Venía en representación de la tribu *Pokanoket*, que hoy llamamos *Wampanoag*. Les habló de otro indio llamado Squanto quien había viajado a Inglaterra.

Los peregrinos le ofrecieron comida a Samoset y le obsequiaron regalos antes de marcharse.

egresó pronto con cinco hombres y las herramientas que habían robado.
es anunció que el gran jefe Massasoit vendría a visitarlos.

El jefe llegó varios días más tarde con un grupo de guerreros, entre ellos Squanto. Compartieron la comida, les obsequiaron regalos a los indios y se llegó a un acuerdo de paz que duró muchos años. Los indios se retiraron, pero Squanto se quedó entre los peregrinos como intérprete.

Squanto les contó que cuando regresaba a Norteamérica de su primer viaje a Londres, había sido secuestrado por el capitán de un barco, quien planeaba venderlo como esclavo, pero logró escaparse y regresar a Inglaterra. Finalmente, lo trajeron a Nueva Inglaterra donde encontró que su tribu, los *Patuxet*, había desaparecido debido a las enfermedades. Él era el único superviviente.

Squanto fue más que un intérprete para los peregrinos. Les enseñó a obtener provecho de la riqueza natural de los bosques. Les mostró donde se encontraban las mejores zonas para la pesca; como cultivar el maíz utilizando el pescado como fertilizante. Sirvió de guía y de intermediario en los trueques de pieles con los indios. Squanto permaneció en Plymouth hasta su muerte en 1622.

El 5 de abril de 1621, el *Mayflower* regresó a Inglaterra. Con la partida del barco, los peregrinos dependerían totalmente de la tierra y de su trabajo para poder subsistir hasta la llegada del próximo navío. El capitán se ofreció a llevar al que quisiera regresar a Inglaterra, pero ni uno solo de los peregrinos aceptó la oferta.

El gobernador John Carver murió en la primavera. Pero para muchos, la llegada de los días más cálidos, produjo un bienestar general y una sensación de alivio. Aunque la mitad de la población había perecido, la colonia Plymouth permanecía en pie.

Por todas partes se percibían señales de constante actividad. Los peregrinos demostraron sus destrezas y pronto aprendieron otras nuevas. Los jóvenes cuidaban los campos, cazaban, hacían estacas de madera para asegurar las vigas y ayudaban a construir viviendas. Tanto los niños como las niñas recogían mejillones y ostras, se ocupaban de cuidar el asado dándole vueltas a las varillas y llenaban los sacos de lino con hojas, pelusillas de maíz o plumas, para hacer colchones. Cuando tenían tiempo libre, los niños aprendían el abecedario y practicaban la lectura estudiando la Biblia y los libros de cánticos y de salmos.

La vida en la colonia tomó un curso normal. Hubo bodas, nacimientos y muertes.

La colonia comenzó a seguir el ritmo de vida de una villa.

La pesca resultó ser abundante y todo parecía indicar que la cosecha produciría lo suficiente para abastecerse durante el invierno que se aproximaba. Aun en pleno verano, los peregrinos habían comenzado a prepararse para el invierno que se acercaba. Desgranaron y almacenaron el maíz; secaron los frutos y conservaron los vegetales en vinagre. Secaron y salaron el pescado y ahumaron la carne. Para festejar esta abundancia, organizaron un Festival de la Cosecha. Esta celebración, que hoy conocemos como el "Día de Acción de Gracias", también fue para agradecer a los indios por la ayuda que les habían prestado a los peregrinos.

La comida era abundante. Aunque la producción de cebada y guisantes (de semillas traídas de Inglaterra) fue pobre, habían conseguido una buena cosecha de habas, maíz y calabaza. Había bacalao y róbalo, asados o guisados. También tenían anguilas, langostas, mejillones y almejas.

Había pudín de calabaza y pan de harina de maíz, uvas y manzanas silvestres, fresas y grosellas secas. Y además, el nuevo gobernador de la colonia, William Bradford, envió a varios hombres a cazar patos, gansos y pavos silvestres.

Los festejos duraron tres días. Los niños se divirtieron jugando. Los hombres participaron en competencias de tiro con el mosquete. Cuando la fiesta estaba más animada, llegó el jefe Massasoit

con noventa hombres, mujeres y niños. Un grupo de hombres se marchó y pronto regresó con cinco venados que se añadieron a la cena. La colonia entera rebosaba de alegría y felicidad.

Este primer "Día de Acción de Gracias" les recordó a los peregrinos todo lo que tenían que agradecer y les infundió la seguridad de que triunfarían. Sus amigos, los indios, se despidieron con renovados votos de amistad y paz — una paz que duró muchos años, hasta que el crecimiento de las colonias creó fricciones entre ambos grupos.

El invierno siguiente fue duro, pero no tan difícil como el primero. Llegó otro barco que traía cerdos y nuevos colonos que llegaron sin provisiones. Sin embargo, el deseo de trabajar juntos y compartir lo que tenían, logró que sobrevivieran ese invierno. Cuando llegó la primavera era evidente que la colonia de Plymouth perduraría.

En los días que siguieron llegaron más barcos de Inglaterra con artículos necesarios como ropa, zapatos, herramientas y mosquetes. También trajeron telas, cuchillos, cuentas de ensartar, alfombras y bisutería para comerciar con los indios. Llegaron algunos productos más cotizados como azúcar, queso y especias y, por último, trajeron ganado. A cambio, los peregrinos enviaron a Inglaterra cargamentos de madera, pescado salado y maíz.

La aventura iniciada por un pequeño grupo de hombres y mujeres valientes se había convertido en algo mucho más grande de lo que ninguno de ellos había podido imaginar. Los peregrinos habían resistido enfermedades, privaciones y toda clase de peligros. La colonia de Plymouth había echado raíces. Con el tiempo, sus hijos serían conocidos como nativos de Nueva Inglaterra o americanos y la semilla que se había sembrado florecería y daría unos frutos extraordinarios.

NOTA DEL AUTOR

Para escribir este libro, consulté numerosas fuentes, incluyendo el informe de William Bradford: "*Of Plymouth Plantation 1620–1647*", y su diario que se encuentra entre los documentos incorporados en *Mourt's Relation* (1622) también de William Bradford (quien sucedió a John Carver como gobernador) y Edward Winslow (el primer asistente del gobernador y más tarde gobernador). Las visitas realizadas a Plymouth, el *Mayflower II* y a la reconstruida Plantación de Plymouth, aportaron importantes conocimientos y datos.

Algunos detalles de las pinturas de N. C. Wyeth difieren de la realidad de los primeros tiempos de Plymouth. Los peregrinos no usaban ni ropa tan sombría ni gorros y cuellos blancos almidonados todos los días. Los muebles que aparecen en la pintura de la cabaña son posiblemente de una época posterior. El ganado no fue traído a Plymouth hasta 1624.

La ortografía en algunos de los escritos antiguos varía, de manera que algunas veces "Plymouth" aparece escrito como "Plimouth", y "Myles" Standish, como "Miles". Los peregrinos utilizaban un calendario que señalaba las fechas con mayor anticipación que los calendarios de hoy día. En este libro se utilizan las fechas registradas por la colonia.

En cuanto a la primera celebración del "Día de Acción de Gracias", llevada a cabo por los peregrinos, los tres días de fiesta reflejan más las tradiciones religiosas de los Separatistas (aunque estos actos solemnes usualmente tenían lugar en la iglesia). También tiene una similitud con los festivales de la cosecha de los romanos, griegos y antiguos hebreos. Así como con el Día de Gracias de los holandeses, y la celebración anual de la cosecha de los ingleses.

Durante los primeros años en América, estos eventos religiosos fueron proclamados por el Consejo de las Colonias o por el nuevo gobierno federal como un evento propio de una comunidad o una religión en particular.

En 1777, el Congreso Continental proclamó la primera fiesta nacional del "Día de Acción de Gracias" — un día de reflexión — para conmemorar la derrota de los ingleses en Saratoga. Más tarde, los presidentes George Washington, John Adams y James Monroe proclamaron festividades de carácter nacional de Acción de Gracias, pero hacia el año 1815, esta costumbre casi había desaparecido.

En 1827, la escritora Sarah Josepha Hale, comenzó una campaña que duró casi cuarenta años para restablecer esta festividad. El 26 de noviembre de 1863, el presidente Abraham Lincoln proclamó fiesta nacional el último jueves del mes de noviembre para celebrar el "Día de Acción de Gracias". En 1939, el presidente Franklin Delano Roosevelt cambió la fecha del cuarto al tercer jueves de noviembre, pero la mayoría del pueblo no estaba contenta con este cambio. En 1941, por resolución del Congreso se restableció la festividad para el cuarto jueves de noviembre.

Hoy, el "Día de Acción de Gracias" nos invita a recordar los logros realizados por los peregrinos y la paz y la amistad que reinaba entre los nativos americanos y los primeros colonizadores. Esto nos debe alentar para tratar de conseguir una armonía general que refleje los ideales de aquellos primeros días de Plymouth.

Robert D. San Souci

ACERCA DEL ARTISTA

Nacido en 1882, en Needham, Massachusetts, Newell Convers Wyeth perteneció a la primera de tres generaciones de una familia de artistas extraordinarios. Influido por sus raíces norteamericanas, su admiración por la obra de Henry David Thoreau, y sus estudios bajo la tutela de Howard Pyle (considerado como el padre de la ilustración americana), N. C. Wyeth fue un consumado artista.

En 1902, Wyeth viajó a Delaware, para estudiar en la pequeña escuela de Pyle. Su trabajo maduró rápidamente, y su primer grabado fue publicado en la portada del *"Saturday Evening Post"* en 1903. La ilustración era de un domador de potros, y Wyeth comenzó a ser conocido como un ilustrador especializado en el oeste americano.

Sin embargo, las ilustraciones más famosas de Wyeth son de los clásicos infantiles tales como *La isla del tesoro, Robin Hood, El último mohicano, y Rip Van Winkle.* Estos volúmenes son muy cotizados hoy día por los coleccionistas. Menos conocidos son otros murales que él pintó para varios clientes.

En 1940 se le comisionó a Wyeth la creación de una serie de murales para la compañía de seguros de Nueva York: *Metropolitan Life Insurance Company.* Él propuso una serie de hechos históricos llamada: "La balada de América" que comenzaría con los peregrinos para continuar con la quimera del oro de California. La compañía *Metropolitan Life* decidió limitar la serie a la Colonia de Plymouth. En estos murales, Wyeth desafió las nociones que existían acerca de los peregrinos como una sociedad intensamente severa, al exponer en sus cuadros la alegría y la belleza de la colonia. Las pinturas revelan la visión romántica y el lirismo: sello distintivo del estilo de Wyeth.

Los dos primeros murales fueron instalados en 1941. Durante los próximos cuatro años, Wyeth amplió su concepto original al incluir escenas de la fauna silvestre de aves, y ciervos, con el fin de transmitir esa paz bucólica que él estaba convencido que los peregrinos habían encontrado en Plymouth.

Wyeth finalizó catorce de los murales, pero antes de que pudiera terminar el resto, murió en un accidente de automóvil el 19 de octubre de 1945.

En 1984, John Creedon, presidente y jefe ejecutivo de *Metropolitan Life,* aprobó un proyecto para limpiar y restaurar los murales. Margaret Watherston, una conocida restauradora de pinturas, fue contratada para conservar los murales que hoy se encuentran en exhibición permanente.

Los murales de *Metropolitan Life* constituyen la labor más importante realizada por Wyeth, y engloban la dimensión total de su visión artística. En ellos se puede apreciar su profundo amor por la naturaleza, por la aventura y por la historia, y por América y todas sus gentes, y su sentido siempre positivo de la experiencia humana.

The names of those which came over first, in ye year .1620.
and were (by the blesing of God) the first beginers, and
(in a sort) the foundation, of all the plantations, and
Colonies, in New-England (And their families.)

8 — m^r John Caruer.
kathrine, his wife.
Desire minter; &
2. man-seruants
John Howland
Roger Wilder.
William Latham, a boy.
& a maid seruant, & a
child y^t was put to him
caled, Jasper More

6 — m^r William Brewster.
Mary his wife, with
2. sons, whose names
were Loue, & Wrasling.
and a boy was put to
him caled Richard More; and another
of his brothers
the rest of his Children
were left behind & came
ouer afterwards.

5 — m^r Edward Winslow
Elizabeth his wife, &
2. men seruants, caled
Georg Sowle, and
Elias Story; also a litle
girle was put to him caled
Ellen, the sister of Richard
More.

2 — William Bradford. and
Dorathy his wife, hauing
but one child, a sone left
behind, who came afterward.

6 — m^r Isaack Allerton, and
Mary his wife; with 3. Children
Bartholmew
Remember, &
Mary. and a seruant boy,
John Hooke.

m^r Samuell fuller, and

---

2 — Captin Myles Standish
and Rose, his wife

4 — m^r Christpher Martin,
and his wife; and 2. seruants,
Salamon prower, and
John Langemore

5 — m^r William Mullines, and his
wife; and 2. Children
Joseph, & priscila; and a seruant
Robart Carter.

6 — m^r ~~White~~ William White, and
Susana his wife; and one sone
caled resolued, and one borne
a ship-bord caled perigréene; &
2. seruants, named
William Holbeck, & Edward Thomson

8 — m^r ~~Hopins~~ Steuen Hopkins, &
Elizabeth his wife; and 2.
Children, caled giles, and
Constanta a doughter; both
by a former wife. And 2. more
by this wife, caled Damaris, &
Oceanus; the last was borne at
sea. And 2. seruants, Called
Edward Doty, and Edward Litster.

1 — m^r Richard Warren, but his
wife and Children were left
behind and came afterwards

4 — John Billinton, and Elen his wife:
and 2. sones John, & francis.

4 — Edward Tillie, and Ann his wife:
and 2. Children that were their

---

2 — Francis Cooke, and his sone John;
But his wife, & other Children came
afterwards

2 — Thomas Rogers, and Joseph his
sone; his other Children came after
wards.

2 — Thomas Tinker, and his wife, and a
sone

2 — John Rigdale; and Alice his
wife.

3 — James Chilton, and his wife, and
Mary their doughter; they had an
other doughter y^t was maried came
afterward.

3 — Edward fuller, and his wife; and
Samuell their sonne.

3 — John Turner, and 2. sones; he
had a doughter came some years
after to Salem, wher she is now
liuing.

3 — Francis Eaton, and Sarah his
wife, and samuell their sone, a yong
Child

10 — Moyses fletcher
John Goodman
Thomas Williams
Digerie preist
Edmond Margeson
peter Browne
Richard Britterige
Richard Clarke
Richard Gardenar
Gilbart Winslow

1 — John Alden was hired for a
Cooper, at South-Hampton wher
the ship victuled; and being
a hopful yongman was